ABE-3242

D0599331

ABE-3242

Chinese American Portraits

Chinese American Portraits

Personal Histories 1828-1988
By Ruthanne Lum McCunn

University of Washington Press
Seattle and London

Library of Congress Cataloging-in-Publication Data

McCunn, Ruthanne Lum.
    Chinese American portraits : personal histories, 1828–1988 / by
Ruthanne Lum McCunn.
        p.   cm.
    Includes bibliographical references and index.
    ISBN 0-295-97552-0 (alk. paper)
    1. Chinese Americans—Biography.   2. Chinese Americans—
Social conditions.   I. Title.
E184.C5M195   1996
305.895'1073—dc20   96-8925
                                                                CIP

A note on transliteration and additional permissions appear on
page 168.

The paper used in this publication meets the minimum
requirements of American National Standard for Information
Sciences—Permanence of Paper for Printed Library Materials,
ANSI Z39.48-1984.

Contents

For
Tsai Nuliang and Judy Yung;
they know the many reasons why.

*In these days one reads and hears much about Chinese diplo-
mats, Chinese persons of high rank, Chinese visitors of promi-
nence, and others, who by reason of wealth and social standing
are interesting to the American people. But of those Chinese who
come to live in this land, to make their homes in America . . .
we hear practically nothing at all. Yet these Chinese, Chinese
Americans I call them, are not unworthy of a little notice.*
—Sui Sin Far
"Chinese Workmen in America"
Independent, July 3, 1913

Preface

Shortly after I began teaching in a small California town, I went to the principal to make a request. I forget what I wanted, but I well remember his response: "You don't have a Chinaman's chance."

I must have looked as astonished as I felt.

"Haven't you heard that expression?" he laughed, aware that I was of Chinese ancestry.

Unable to speak, I shook my head, no.

"Chinese in America used to have such a tough time of it that the likelihood of their survival was next to nothing. So, to have a Chinaman's chance is to have no chance at all," he said, giving me a concise summary of Chinese American history, a taste of being Chinese in America today.

Since then I have spent ten years researching the Chinese American experience—past and present—in documents, newspapers, memoirs, books, personal papers, interviews, and photographs. What I have sought, and share with you here, are women and men who have fought against the odds. They have not always won. Nor are they necessarily heroic. Being human, they have flaws. But they have refused to give up the struggle—and they have endured.

◈ Pioneers ◈

Yung Wing 1828–1912
From Nam Ping Village, China, to Springfield, Massachusetts, and Hartford, Connecticut (Courtesy Connecticut Historical Society)

Yung Wing and
the Chinese Educational Mission

Yung Wing, Yale University, Class of 1854, was the first person of Chinese ancestry to graduate from an American college. As early as 1818, Chinese were studying at the Foreign Mission School in Cornwall, Connecticut, but none had ever completed a degree.

Wing's own diploma was hard won. Unlike other Yale freshmen, he had only studied fifteen months of Latin, twelve months of Greek, and ten months of mathematics. Besides struggling to keep up with his classmates, he had to support himself by doing the marketing and waiting on tables for a boarding club and by working as an assistant librarian for one of the debating societies. His poverty, nationality, and natural reserve kept him from participating much in the social life of his college, and he often felt isolated and lonely.

None of these difficulties were new to Wing. Born in the southern Chinese village of Nam Ping in 1828, he had begun his education at the age of seven. A boarder in a missionary school in the Portuguese colony of Macau, he had often cried himself to sleep and had even tried to run away. Then, after his father died, he dropped out of school to help his older brother support their mother, sister, and younger brother. Only twelve, he hawked candy, gleaned rice after the reapers, and worked in a printing office for more than a year before a sympathetic missionary doctor helped him resume his education at the Morrison School in Hong Kong.

The principal, the Reverend S. R. Brown, was highly regarded by his students, and when he was forced by ill health to return to America in 1847, Wing and two other boys accompanied him. Brown placed them in the care of his mother at Monson, Massachusetts, where they attended the Monson Academy.

The plan was for the boys to return to China when they graduated from the preparatory school. One, too sickly to stay, returned to Hong Kong after only a year. The second left to pursue medical studies in Scotland in 1849. Wing resolved to go to Yale, the college from which Brown had graduated.

Since his father's death, Wing's education had been paid for by missionaries, and if he had agreed to become one, his support at Yale would have been guaranteed. Though a sincere Christian, he refused: "The calling of a missionary is not the only sphere in life where one can do the most good [and] I would not allow my poverty to gain the upper hand and compel me to barter away my inward convictions of duty for a temporary mess of potage."

His commitment was to help regenerate China through a scheme that would give Chinese youths the same educational advantages he had enjoyed. As he wrote Yale's president on accepting his diploma: "I shall bear it for China and the Chinese and regard it . . . as an encouragement to [them] to come out and try great possibilities and Western Literature, Science and Religion."

For the next seventeen years Wing labored in China to make his dream, the education of Chinese youths in America, a reality. Government officials were unreceptive. Humiliated by repeated defeats and concessions to foreign powers, they equated his proposal for Western education with "bowing down" to the hated foreigners. Yet the country was dependent on foreign experts for shipbuilding, engineering, and other technology. Finally, in 1871, a few officials—recognizing that Chinese had to become technically proficient themselves—gave Wing the support necessary to launch the Chinese Educational Mission.

Every year, for four consecutive years, a detachment of thirty male students would be sent to New England. The students would study for fifteen years before returning to China, and their age, upon return, would be no more than thirty. Chinese teachers were to be provided to keep up their knowledge of Chinese. And, most important to the officials who sanctioned the project, "As the young students grow up, those who are qualified should be sent to West Point and the Naval Academy as cadets for advanced training."

Parents were suspicious of the government's offer to educate their sons and pay them a modest stipend as well. They were reluctant to be separated from their children for so many years, and they worried about their children's reception abroad. One boy's parents withdrew their permission when villagers told them that wild men in America would skin the children alive, graft the skins of dogs onto their bodies, and exhibit them as they would "some uncommon animal."

In order to fill the first complement of thirty students, Wing personally had to scour the southern districts, where people were familiar with foreign traders.

THE LIVING CHINESE FAMILY.
Arrived in New York April 1850, in the Ship IANTHE Capt Johnson from Canton.
Exhibited under the auspices of P. T. BARNUM Proprietor of AMERICAN and CHINESE MUSEUMS New York and BARNUMS MUSEUM Philadelphia.

Chinese villagers' fears that their children might be exhibited like "some uncommon animal" were not unfounded. In 1850, P. T. Barnum's exhibition of a normal Chinese family in his traveling show drew thousands. Even the most commonplace actions of Chinese—burying their dead or eating—drew large crowds.
(Top photo courtesy Chinese Women of America Project, Chinese Culture Foundation of San Francisco; middle photo courtesy Montana Historical Society; bottom photo courtesy South Dakota State Historical Society)

Of the four groups that left for America between 1872 and 1875, ninety percent were from Kwangtung, the province from which Chinese had been emigrating for two decades.

To screen and prepare prospective students, the Chinese government established a preparatory school in Shanghai. One student, Wen Bing Chung, described the school as "much study and little play. The curriculum contained few subjects, which had, however, to be learned well and thoroughly. Memorizing the classics was compulsory. Science was not taught. Shouting one's lessons at the top of the voice was considered the proper way to learn."

Another student, Lee Yan Phou, wrote of his introduction to English at the school: "The letters sounded rather funny, I must say. The letter *r* was the hardest one to pronounce, but I soon learned to give it, with a peculiar roll of the tongue even. We were taught to read and write English and managed by means of primers and phrase books to pick up a limited knowledge of the language."

After a year's study, the students were examined in English and the best thirty were selected to go to America. Their proficiency in Chinese, their deportment, and their general record were also taken into account. For those who passed, like Yan Phou, "There was great rejoicing among our friends and kindred. For the cadet's gilt button and rank were conferred on us, which, like the first literary degree, was a step toward fortune, rank and influence. Large posters were pasted up at the front doors of our homes, informing the world in gold characters of the great honor which had come to the family."

The students were instructed on how to behave in the presence of officials and trained in the rules of etiquette. Then, after ceremonial visits to pay their respects to the head of the Shanghai Customs (technically their Chief Examiner) and the American Consul General, they said good-bye to family and friends and set sail for America.

To make the necessary arrangements for the students' accommodations and education, Wing preceded them by a month. Trusted friends and professors from his own years in America suggested he place the students by twos and threes in families throughout New England so that they would learn English and Western customs more readily. Wing, following this advice, called for volunteer families. The response was so enthusiastic that there were more than enough families for all the boys who came during the next four years.

Wing had selected Hartford, Connecticut, for the project's headquarters. As each contingent of thirty boys arrived, he assigned them to families that would be their guardians during their term in America. "It was my good fortune," Yan Phou remembered, "to be placed into the hands of a most motherly lady in Springfield. She came after us in a hack. As I was pointed out to her, she put her arms around me and kissed me. This made the rest of the boys laugh, and perhaps I got rather red in the face; however, I would say nothing to show my embarrassment. But that was the first kiss I ever had since my infancy."

Students and guardians were mutually curious. The boys wondered how American males could walk or run in such tight-fitting jackets and pants. They were shocked by the impropriety of American women walking arm-in-arm with men, and they found American voices shrill. Their New England families were confused by the boys' long queues and silk robes. One of the guardians, Eugene C. Gardener, later wrote, "They seemed like innocent, helpless wild animals of the woods that ought to be sent immediately back to their mothers."

The students' limited English created a few problems initially. In one family, the boys, when told to get ready for Sunday school, only caught the word "school" and were shocked to find themselves marched into a church. Since they had been warned to withstand attempts to Christianize them, the boys raced out of the church, to the consternation of their hosts.

Those who were advanced enough in English were sent to schools. The rest were given private tutoring at home. As Yan Phou explained, "We learned English by object lessons. At table we were always told the names of certain dishes, and then assured that if we could not remember the name we were not to partake of that article of food. Taught by this method, our progress was rapid and surprising."

According to Gardener, "After a year or two of home instruction by no means confined to books, they became in public or private school the peers of their contemporaries in age who had been studying in the same schools

The Hartford and Springfield newspapers repeatedly referred to the Chinese Educational Mission students as being "all from the higher classes of Chinese gentry and nobility," "high caste," and "of course of a different class from the Chinese so well known by their service as launders, who are mostly Cantonese." In fact, over half the students came from the same province and economic background—and sometimes even the same family—as the "launders." The major differences between them were the opportunities offered or denied.

The first detachment of students on their arrival in Hartford. (Courtesy Connecticut Historical Society)

Some of the same students shortly before their recall. (Courtesy Connecticut Historical Society)

In the late 1870s, Boston merchants raised $8,750 to establish a "Chinese teachership" at Harvard University. The course in Mandarin would be intense—eight hours a day, five days a week—and it would be open to anyone, women excepted. The search for an educated man willing to leave China took longer than expected. Finally, in 1879, Ko Kun Hua (top)—a Mandarin who had held "the position of writer" at the British Consulate in Ningpo for fifteen years—was settled upon as an ideal choice. He was a scholar, familiar with foreigners, and a good teacher.

Accompanied by his wife, children (bottom), a female servant, and an interpreter, Ko set sail for America. Their reception in Cambridge was warm, and the family settled into a small house near the university. Ko held classes every day. He wore Chinese official dress and required his students to pay him the same respect that was due a teacher in China. During his tenure he only taught five students, but "with satisfactory results"; and he wrote a collection of poetry, part of which he translated and annotated in English before his death from pneumonia in 1881.

The local newspapers reported his death with respect: "Upon his arrival here in 1879, Professor Ko could not speak a word in English, but at his decease, he conversed in our language with a good degree of facility. He was a man of very refined manners, simple and modest in his demeanor, and of a remarkably lovable character." The instructors at Harvard raised $3,763 for the support of Ko's family, and they returned to China. (Courtesy Harvard University Archives)

since infancy. There was no occasion to teach them morals or manners; they taught us these things by example, if not by precept, especially in the matter of consistently practicing what we preached."

The boys captured many prizes in the local schools and their work was exhibited in the Educational Pavilion at the 1876 International Exhibition in Pennsylvania. China's representative to the Exhibition, Li Kuei, was impressed by the students he met. "Some who have been to the States about one year can unbelievably speak pretty good English," he wrote. "They care for one another and interact with Westerners in elegant manners."

Teased about the long Chinese gowns and queues that "made them look like girls," the boys assumed American dress and coiled their queues around their heads or hid them under their coats. They were popular at church socials and dances, and they learned American games, often playing on their school teams. One boy, Liang Tun-yen, pitched for Hartford High School and then Yale. A southpaw, he had an erratic delivery that became the terror of local teams, especially since it was accomplished by "the most surprising contortions of the body while his queue was describing a series of mathematical curves in the air."

On Saturdays and during school vacations, the students pursued their Chinese curriculum in preparation for the Chinese Civil Service examination that they would have to take when they went home. Classes were held at the Chinese Educational Mission headquarters in Hartford, which the boys nicknamed "hell house." The building contained classrooms and boarding facilities for seventy-five students and a central hall with tablets of Confucius and the Emperor, to which the students were required to pay their respects on special occasions. At regular intervals they were also gathered as a group to listen to a Chinese Commissioner read the Emperor's edicts.

While Wing was responsible for the students' foreign education and housing, a different Commissioner was in charge of their Chinese education. There were two Commissioners during the life of the Chinese Educational Mission, and both were conservative Confucianists who disapproved of the boys playing baseball, converting to Christianity, and "making love" to American girls. Wing defended the boys, thereby confirming the Commissioners' opinion that he was hopelessly Westernized. They considered Wing's marriage to Mary Kellogg in 1876 proof of their worst fears, and they accused him of undermining their efforts to maintain the students' native language, culture, and identity.

Kwong Ki Chiu, the official translator and interpreter for the Chinese Educational Mission from 1875 to 1881, compiled A Dictionary of English Phrases with Illustrative Sentences, *which was published in 1881. Also in circulation at the time was* An English-Chinese Phrase Book *for Chinese laborers. These two volumes illustrate the gulf between the experiences of the students and laborers. The dictionary included terms necessary for the stock exchange, Latin and French phrases, and historical sketches, while the phrase book taught sentences crucial for survival: "He cheated me out of my wages." "They were lying in ambush." "He was strangled to death by a man." "The confession was extorted from him by force. . . ." (Courtesy Connecticut Historical Society)*

The Chinese Educational Mission's baseball club, the Orientals, in front of the Mission's headquarters in Hartford, Connecticut. (Courtesy Washington State University Library, Pullman)

Chung Mun Yew, nicknamed "Munny," twice piloted the Yale rowing team to victory over Harvard. At a Harvard-Yale meeting many years later, a Harvard man expressed doubt as to whether Munny had even seen a race. Unruffled, Munny admitted he had never seen a Harvard crew row because they were always behind him. (Courtesy Yale University Archives)

Actually, Wing knew from personal experience the difficulties and the importance of retaining the Chinese language. While a student at Yale, he had written a missionary friend in China for Chinese books because "No one now talks with me in Chinese, and I am fast losing especially the written or literal part." Having been educated entirely in missionary schools, Wing lacked a firm enough grounding to maintain the language on his own, and when he returned to China in 1854 he discovered to his chagrin that he had to relearn the Cantonese dialect in order to communicate. He fully understood that if the boys were to succeed on their return to China, they could not afford to lose their native language. Not only did he want them to keep up with their Chinese, he also encouraged Yale to establish a chair for a Chinese professorship.

Remembering his own loneliness, Wing was glad to see the boys' social success. Unlike the Commissioners, he was confident the boys' rapid acculturation would not weaken their loyalty to China. Before his graduation from Yale, Wing had become a naturalized American citizen, and, years earlier, had converted to Christianity. Yet he had devoted his whole life to China, firmly believing the scripture, "If any provide not for his own, and specially for those of his own house, he hath denied the faith, and is worse than an infidel."

Not all the members of the Chinese Educational Mission's staff shared the Chinese Commissioners' opposition to Western culture. One teacher and his family attended church faithfully. According to the local papers, they all spoke English and became "favorites in society"; one son even wrote poetry in English, some of which was published in the *Springfield Republican*. And Kwong Ki Chiu, the interpreter for the Mission from 1875 to 1881, spent his free time putting together an English-Chinese dictionary that included American slang and learning the art of creating stereotype printing plates from a local photographer.

But it was the Commissioners who were responsible for sending reports to China, and they grew increasingly negative, alarming the conservatives who were replacing the reformers that had helped found the Chinese Educational Mission. The Chinese officials ordered Wing to tighten discipline and were furious when he did not. Nevertheless, it was neither the Commissioners nor the conservatives who caused the breakup of the project, but the American government.

During the mid-1870s, American politicians had singled out Chinese laborers as scapegoats for the country's economic depression. By 1879, punitive ordinances and violence against the Chinese on the Pacific Coast were common, and Congress passed the first Chinese Exclusion Act. President Hayes vetoed it. But the State Department, giving in to anti-Chinese sentiment, refused to admit qualified Chinese Educational Mission students to the Military Academy at West Point and the Naval Academy in Annapolis.

The denial was contrary to the Burlingame Treaty of 1868, which promised that "Chinese subjects shall enjoy all the privileges of the public educational institutions under the control of the government of the United States." But the State Department was adamant, making it impossible for the Chinese Educational Mission to continue. The Chinese government ordered the staff and students home.

The recall was a bitter pill for the students. Out of the original 120, there remained 101 (3 had died, 16 had been sent home for insubordination, getting into debt, or cutting their queues). Most of the remaining students were just beginning the college educations toward which they had worked for so many years. Some were only one or two years from graduation.

They called a mass meeting and delegated representatives to ask Wing to intercede on their behalf with the American and Chinese governments. Their American instructors, guardians, and friends also sent letters of protest. But all attempts to stop the recall were to no avail. Wing was able to help his nephew, Yung Kwai, remain by secretly providing the necessary funds for him to complete his education at Yale. Everyone else had to go.

The return journey in 1881 was not without at least one moment of triumph. While waiting for their steamer in San Francisco, the Chinese Educational Mission's baseball team received a challenge from the Oakland baseball team. One of the students present, Wen Bing Chung, recalled the game forty-two years later:

> The Oakland men imagined that they were going to have a walk-over with the Chinese. Who had seen Celestials playing baseball? But the Oakland nine got the shock of their life as soon as they attempted to connect with the deliveries of the Chinese pitcher; the fans were equally surprised at the strange phenomenon—Chinese playing their national ball game and showing the Yankees some of the thrills in the game. Unimaginable! All the same, the Chinese walloped them, to the great

In 1919, Liang Tun Yen sent his thirteen-year-old son, Che Chiang, to live with his best friend from high school and Yale, Martin Welles. When the boy arrived in Hartford, a reporter noted that Che's "European dress is much more like that of a young Continental dandy than of an American or English boy." But Che soon proved himself "all boy." In fact, his letters from school were so full of football that his father wrote Welles: "Please advise {Che} to pay more attention to his studies than to his games—to prepare himself for that greater football game of life; otherwise he will be a football instead of a football player." (Courtesy Connecticut Historical Society)

Many of the students who followed the Chinese Educational Mission were also pampered, traveling in luxury to universities all across America. (Courtesy Washington State Historical Society)

rejoicing of their comrades and fellow countrymen. This was the last baseball game the Chinese team played, for they never got together again afterwards.

The welcome the students received in China was cold. After being made much of in America for so many years, it was particularly hard to bear. As described by Wong Kai-kah in a letter to his American guardian:

One solitary man came aboard to receive us—our postal manager, Mr. Luk. . . . We came to the Harbour Master's house, and after roll-call and a substantial supper, not elaborately prepared, we were dispatched with a detachment of Chinese marines acting as a guard over us to prevent our escaping from the grasp of our paternal government (?) to the "Knowledge Wishing Institution" inside the city behind the court of the Shanghai Taotai. Your Western imagination is too sublime to conceive a place so vile as this so-called institution; you may have read about Turkish prisons or

Andersonville Horrors, but compared with this they must have been enviable places. . . .

After four days' groaning and complaining, we were summoned to hold audience with the highest official in Shanghai. In three bodies we were mustered with enough guards to keep a regiment in quiet subjection; we commenced our journey amidst crowds of spectators whose comments were far from being flattering, and marched through piles of dirt and filth which commanded the entrance of the Taotai Yamen.

After prostrating themselves, they were finally dismissed and able to return to their homes. But as Wen Bing Chung pointed out, "Then commenced their life battles in earnest."

The former students encountered prejudice and strong opposition from members of the literary and official classes, who declared that they had become "foreign devils" and were of "no use to the country." Westernized they were. But through patience and perseverance, they gradually convinced the government of their integrity, loyalty, and patriotism.

Many built distinguished careers in the service of China, constructing railroads and telegraph lines, developing coal mines, becoming China's first modern trained army and navy officers, or filling the ranks of her consular and diplomatic service. But a few, bitterly resentful of their unjust treatment, returned to America as soon as they could find the means to do so.

One of them, Jang Ting Seong, stowed away in a junk that he thought was bound for Java, where he hoped to find passage for America. Instead, the junk was an official one carrying a fellow Chinese Educational Mission student to his post in Korea. The former student helped Jang Ting Seong secure passage to America, where he became well known as a consulting engineer.

Another, Chang Hong-yen, returned to Columbia Law School with the help of his brother, a successful merchant in Honolulu. A leader of his class, he graduated in 1886. However, he was prevented from taking the examinations to become a member of the King's County Bar "by the provisions of the law relating to Chinese emigration." This final hurdle was overcome when a well-known judge became interested in Chang's case and succeeded in securing the passage of a special bill in the New York Legislature on May 21, 1887. The bill authorized the Supreme Court of the state to "waive [Chang's] alienage" and to admit and license him to practice as an attorney and counselor in all courts of the state. Later, when Hong-yen moved to California, he was not permitted to practice there, and he worked as an interpreter for a bank and then for the Chinese diplomatic service.

The friendships with New Englanders endured, some through several generations. Many former Chinese Educational Mission students sent their children, daughters as well as sons, back to their "American families" for their educations. So intimate were the relationships which developed that a letter to one host began, "Dear Old Bald Headed Angel."

The men who, as children, had nicknamed the Mission headquarters "hell house" now insisted that their children in America keep up their Chinese. But the new generation was as irrepressible as the old. One boy was on the basketball and football teams, played tennis, learned to ride, collected stamps, and conducted magic shows!

Nevertheless, as one Westerner observed, "The high jinks [and] the 'rah-rah-ing' for everybody and everything did not entirely succeed in obscuring the fact that these keen, wide-awake youths, with their easy manners and smiling faces, meant business. And what they make of [China] is going to depend a good deal upon what they make of their opportunities here at study."

As for Yung Wing, he returned to his family in America after accompanying the students home. In 1895 he went again to China and attempted to establish a national banking system and to build a railroad. These and other schemes failed, and he returned permanently to the United States in 1902. He remained interested in reforming China until his death in 1912.

Mary Bong 1880–1958
From Kwangtung, China, to Sitka, Alaska (Courtesy Special Collections Division, University of Washington Libraries)

Mary Bong,
Frontierswoman

Traditionally, Tankas (the boat people of south-eastern China) were born, lived, and died without ever setting foot on land. But when Mary Bong was six years old, she and her parents were forced to go ashore to look for work.

During the mulberry season, Mary and her mother, like thousands of other women and children, stripped the leaves from mulberry trees and packed them into baskets. Intersecting the densely planted fields were narrow canals where hundreds of men, including Mary's father, paddled little boats back and forth to pick up the baskets. When the harvest was over, the family moved to the orange groves and then to the rice fields. In between, they fished.

According to Mary, "When I was nine I decided that wasn't the life for me, so the first chance I got I ran away from my riverboat home."

Talk in the port cities was that those who dared cross the Pacific would find mountains of gold, and Mary, working long, hard hours at manual labor, saved every penny she could for the fare. Since 1870, however, all Chinese women wishing to emigrate to America had first to prove their "correct habits and good character" to the United States Commissioner of Immigration. The American Consul in Hong Kong, charged with the initial examination of the women, permitted them to purchase tickets only if convinced of their good character. Even with his approval, women were often refused landing or detained at ports of entry and forced to file petitions of habeas corpus (with hefty bonds of over $1,000) before being released. After passage of the 1882 Exclusion Act, almost the only women admitted were the wives of merchants.

Mary therefore bought passage to Vancouver, Canada, where she schemed successfully to marry a merchant, Ah Bong, who operated the Sang Wo Bakery and Restaurant in Sitka, Alaska. Finally, on October 12, 1895, she arrived in Sitka, realizing her dream. She was fifteen years old.

Sitka, the capital of the Territory, was a pioneer settlement consisting of a trading post, gambling hall, saloons, and a scattering of other frame buildings. Over half the population was Tlingit Indians, the rest a mix of Russians, Swedes, Norwegians, English, Finns, and Chinese. Mary was the first, and only, Chinese woman in Sitka and perhaps Alaska.

Since she had picked up some English in Vancouver, Mary took over the management of her husband's restaurant. Many of the customers were young men from the mining camp on Chichagof Island. When they came into town "to make whoopee" and showed up drunk at the restaurant, Mary would take their money away, leaving them thirty or forty dollars to spend for a good time.

"In a few days they'd show up sober and looking sheepish," she recalled. "Then they'd say, 'Mary, will you stake me to meals until I can get a boat back to the mine?' I would tell them okay, and when they were ready to leave I'd return their pokes, minus the prices of the meals they'd owe me for. That way they didn't go back broke."

She became friendly with the Tlingit Indians, learning their language. There was no doctor in Sitka, and after giving birth to two girls of her own, Mary often acted as midwife for the Tlingit women, never losing a single baby. In return, they taught her how to make trinkets and bracelets out of silver.

Then, in 1902, Ah Bong died and she lost the restaurant. Katherine, her elder daughter, was six and in school, but Anna was only a year old. While Mary did housework, a friendly barber kept Anna in a room at the rear of his store, feeding and changing the baby between customers. At first she earned only twenty-five cents a day, then fifty cents, then a dollar. Since the barber refused to charge for babysitting, Mary was able to manage. After five years, she even paid off her house. A few months later, she remarried.

Her new husband, Fred Johnson, was of Swedish-Finnish descent. He was not the kind of man to settle in one place, and after their wedding, Mary took her two girls to Seattle and enrolled them in boarding school, where she hoped they would receive the education she never had. Then, back in Alaska, she joined her husband at the Chichagof mine.

This mine was extremely rich, yielding several million dollars of gold. Fred had helped put in the first tunnel, and he taught Mary how to handle blasting powder. She also worked underground, shoveling ore

THE CHINESE JUNK "KEYING"

CAPT. KELLETT

As she appeared in New York harbour July 18th 1847. 212 days from Canton. — 720 tons burthen.

DIMENSIONS		
Length	· ·	160 Feet
Breadth of Beam	· ·	25¾
Depth of Hold	· ·	12
Hoop from the Water	·	45
Bow	· ·	30
Rudder. Weight	· ·	7¾ to 8 Tons

Mainsail	· · · · 9 Tons
Mainmast 75 Feet long from Deck	
Upper Mainyard	67 Feet long
Lower "	60 "
720 Tons Burthen.	
The Ship is Built of Teak Wood.	

Chinese have a long tradition as skillful and courageous seamen and fishermen. On July 10, 1847, the Kee Ying, *a 720-ton junk, reached New York after a 212-day voyage from Hong Kong. During her four-month tour of New York, Providence, and Boston, she attracted over 50,000 paying visitors. Some of the crew are thought to have jumped ship and settled on the East Coast. (Courtesy Museum of the City of New York)*

into cars. When she smashed a finger so that the bone stuck out through the skin, she simply worked the skin over the flesh and bone and then sewed up the wound herself. "No time to fuss over smashed fingers," she explained. But she did allow the company to talk her into going back above ground to cook for the men.

With their savings, she and Fred started a dairy in 1911 at Sawmill Creek, seven miles out of Sitka. They hacked a clearing out of the wilderness and built a log cabin for themselves and another one for the cows. "I can swing an axe or use a saw the same as any man, and no one has to go with me when I go hunting," Mary said. The dairy's location, however, was impractical, since the milk had to be taken into town in a small boat. Storms and rough water frequently prevented deliveries, and after a few years of struggle, they sold out.

For a while Mary and Fred tried prospecting and trapping. "It was an interesting experience, but we decided it was a slow, hard way to make money, and we didn't need any more experience fighting freezing weather, with the boat icing up and all that tugging and lugging that goes with the job, so we quit."

In 1917, the first salmon cannery was established in Sitka. During the salmon season, gangs of Chinese laborers were brought in under contract to canneries all over Alaska. They gutted the fish and prepared them for canning, often making the cans and weaving the seines for catching the fish as well. Commercial fishing became Sitka's main industry, and Fred bought a cabin troller.

Mary became the first woman troller in the area. She had an eighteen-foot open boat, and she trolled alone, starting at dawn, fishing all day, then coming in to sell her catch for three cents a pound. On foggy days, she would set a compass course so she would not get lost. But the fog sometimes thickened until she could hardly

Chinese pioneer women worked in a variety of occupations including mining, fishing, gardening, washing, clerking, and cooking. Ah Yuen, a cook during the peak of the mining era, lived in the boomtowns of San Francisco, Denver, and Park City before settling in Evanston, Wyoming, where she was also known as "China Mary." Because of the scarcity of Chinese women, she was able to marry a young and wealthy Chinese miner many years her junior. In fact, she had been married twice before, each time to a wealthy miner, and she outlived this third, and last, husband as well. An enthusiastic gambler, she lost her several fortunes and died in poverty at the age of 110 in 1939. (Courtesy Denice Wheeler)

see to bring in her catch. Sea lions often came so close to her skiff that when they dove, the waves would almost capsize her. When it got rough, the boat would take on water and she would have to bail fast to keep from sinking.

"Anyone who wants to fish for a living in this country can't run for shelter every time it gets rough. If he does, he won't be in the fishing business long," she said. Nevertheless, there was at least one occasion when the weather kept everyone out of the water except Mary. She made a good catch and "returned all smiles, but were the faces of the other trollers red!"

In the early twenties, Mary and Fred decided to try fox farming. They purchased an island twenty miles from Sitka and turned several pairs of blue foxes loose on it. Since they could not afford to hire any help, they built their log cabin themselves, and they cooked feed for the foxes from fish that they caught. During the first few years, they pelted only a few in order to build up their breeding stock. Poachers were trapping the foxes, however; even though Mary, armed with a gun, patrolled part of the island, it was too big for her to cover entirely. They tried moving to another island, but it had no fresh water, and eventually they gave up the farm.

It must have sometimes seemed to Mary that she had traded a hard life in China for an equally hard life in Alaska. At seventy she was still working—as official matron of the federal jail in Sitka—and considering purchasing a small boat so that she could troll for salmon. Nevertheless, when she was asked about China, she said, "I'll never go back. China seems like a faraway dream to me." And when the Exclusion Act was repealed in 1943 and Chinese once again had the right to become naturalized citizens, Mary took out citizenship papers so she could vote.

In the spring of 1958, she was admitted to the Pioneers Home Hospital, a combination retirement and nursing home for longtime residents of Alaska. When she died a few weeks later, she was buried in the Pioneers Cemetery. Like many others buried there, her history contains gaps and questions that can never be answered. We don't even know her birth name. "Mary" was acquired in Vancouver, "Bong" from her first husband, and in Alaska, she is simply remembered as "China Mary."

Lalu Nathoy, a Mongolian, was brought to Idaho in 1872 as a slave. After a few years, she was won in a poker game by Charlie Bemis, a saloon keeper, who set her free. She saved his life twice—first by using her crochet hook to dig out bullet fragments that had shattered in his cheek, and then by dragging him out of a burning cabin. They married and settled on the banks of the Salmon River in an area not unlike her childhood home. Renowned for her hospitality, generosity, and extraordinary nursing skills, she is remembered in Idaho today by her Western name, Polly Bemis. (Courtesy Idaho State Historical Society)

Lai Ngan was only fourteen when relatives arranged for her marriage to Lee Kwong in 1883. Both were members of the Chinese Opera Company in San Francisco. But Lee Kwong, a restless dreamer, could not stay in one place long, and he depended on Lai Ngan to support them and their children while he prospected near Hermosillo, Mexico. Leaving the children in the care of her friend, Doña Ramona García (left), Lai Ngan (right) worked in a Chinese-owned shoe factory. One day, a rent collector arrived at her house, and Lai Ngan discovered her husband had sold the home that she had bought out of her wages. Undaunted, she brandished a stick and chased the collector out, shouting, "This is my house and I don't care how many times he has sold it, it's mine." The man never came back.

In 1905 the family moved to Nogales, Arizona (bottom), where Lai Ngan ran another grocery while her husband sold lottery tickets. (Courtesy Marian Lee Lim Collection, Arizona Historical Society)

Lue Gim Gong 1858–1925
From Lung On Village, China, to North Adams, Massachusetts, and DeLand, Florida (Courtesy Mary Kathryn Green McCarthy)

Lue Gim Gong,
Horticulturist

An early morning mist shrouded Lung On Village. But Lue Gim Gong, afraid it was not enough to hide his escape, dared not leave the added shield of high grasses for the dirt path. Mud clung to his cloth shoes, dew drenched his cotton jacket and pants, and he shivered with cold and fear. His departure from the same village sixteen years earlier had been quite different—a blaze of sunshine and noisy farewells. Then he had been a boy of thirteen with a hunger for learning that neither his mother nor the village schoolteacher could satisfy. Now he was a sick man past his prime, a thief stealing his family honor. And only the knowledge that each step was taking him closer to "Mother Fanny" gave him the courage, the strength, to press on.

Lue had met Mother Fanny when he joined her Sunday school class at Calvin T. Sampson's shoe factory in North Adams, Massachusetts. A year earlier, Sampson had broken a strike of the nation's largest and most militant union, The Secret Order of St. Crispin, by bringing in 75 Chinese workers from San Francisco. There were fewer than 100 Chinese in the eastern states, and the crowd that met "Sampson's Chinese" at the station on June 13, 1870, was almost as curious as it was angry.

Taking no chances, however, Sampson hired thirty armed constables who cordoned off the train platform and shielded the Chinese (almost all teenage boys) from hurled stones as they marched the few blocks to a one-story building behind the factory. This building would be their home for the duration of their three-year contracts—and their prison during the first few weeks, when it was too dangerous for them to leave.

As Sampson had intended, his recruitment of Chinese workers broke the union as well as the strike. While the Chinese worked in the assembly and pegging room, more than 200 nonunion workers, most of them new immigrants from Europe and Canada, were hired to replace the Crispins in other areas of the factory. The following year there were no protests when Sampson brought in fifty more Chinese workers, among them Lue Gim Gong, or Lue, as he came to be known.

Sampson's idea of hiring Chinese workers was not original. The May 1869 issue of *Hide and Leather Inter-est*, a journal for manufacturers, had urged the creation of a national organization of employers to import immigrant labor, particularly Chinese, as strikebreakers. The editor of the North Adams newspaper agreed, but noted in an editorial on July 15, 1869: "We should exclude the Mongolians from this country altogether, or give them the rights of humanity after we have permitted them to come here. . . . Christianize and citizenize the Chinese by the touch of human kindness, and we shall succeed, for never yet did Christian effort fail."

The town's Methodist and Baptist ministers therefore organized a Sunday school to teach the Chinese to speak, read, and write English. They also taught simple arithmetic and "plenty of religion." Lue's teacher, Fanny Burlingame, came from a family of staunch Baptists. Forty-four years old, she was a brilliant mathematician and botanist and had been educated at the Wesleyan Young Ladies' Seminary in Macon, Georgia. She was, however, restricted by ill health to living at home and tutoring college aspirants in a little schoolhouse her father, a successful merchant, had built for her in their garden.

Struck by Lue's bright eyes, inquiring mind, and keen intelligence, Fanny quickly singled him out from her other Sunday school students. She extended his lessons from Sunday afternoons in the factory workers' dining room to evening sessions in her little school. Then she began to bring him into her home.

In his village, Lue had worked with his mother in the orange groves, where she taught him how to cross-pollinate blossoms and graft stock. In the Burlingame gardens and hothouse, he worked with Fanny's father and eldest sister, Phoebe, testing, eliminating, and replacing poor stock. Lue's parents had only been able to send him to the village school for three years. Under Fanny's tutelage, he completed the equivalent of at least a high school education. Not surprisingly, while most of the other Chinese left North Adams after their contracts expired, Lue remained.

By then his relationship with Fanny had evolved from teacher and student to mother and son, and he was calling her Mother Fanny. Still working at the shoe factory, he spent all his free time at the Burlingame

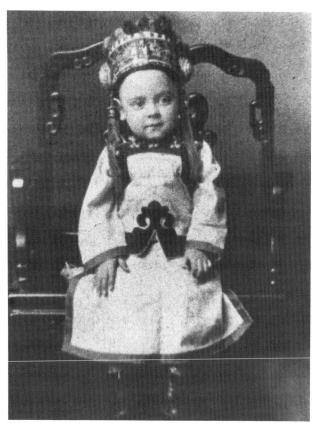

Usually, taking a Chinese child into a white family was considered an act of Christian charity, and no one questioned these informal adoptions. Chinese couples who took in non-Chinese children, however, often had them taken away by the authorities. George Lee Reynolds was a month old when a Chinese couple in Portland, Oregon, adopted him. "I don't know who my biological parents are, so I think I was pretty lucky," he said. "{My mother} dyed my hair, dyed my eyebrows to make me look Chinese. But she couldn't do anything about my blue eyes! {And} there were do-gooders, you know, prying into our affairs. They tried three or four times to take me away from my foster parents, to stick me in an orphan's home. But somehow my foster father had some kind of proof." (Courtesy Christine Richardson)

house, the YMCA reading room, and the First Baptist Church, where he was baptized. He also cut his queue and adopted Western clothing and manners.

Then, in 1886, he was diagnosed as consumptive. It was thought that walking backwards up the hill just outside of town could cure the disease. But Lue had watched Fanny's youngest sister die from consumption despite the walks. Hoping his life might be prolonged in the warmer climate of southern China, he went back to Lung On.

He found the village and the age-old beliefs intolerable. One of Lue's brothers, who had also been to America, had brought back a water pump. By pumping water uphill, he had been able to plant orange trees where only wild grass had grown. But when the trees came into bearing, the farmers in the next village had complained that the trees blocked their *fung-shui,* wind and water, and they had razed the grove. Lue's brother accepted the judgment. Lue could not.

Nor could he understand his mother's insistence that he marry. To him, taking a bride and fathering a son when he knew he was sick and could soon be dead was wrong. But his mother saw only the need for a son to make offerings to Lue's spirit. Ignoring his protests, she sought the help of a matchmaker and selected a bride. Lue had passively observed the betrothal agreement and exchange of gifts, but on his wedding morning, he finally took action, stealing away from the village under cover of the pre-dawn mist.

For the shame he brought on his family, Lue's name was struck from the family register. Years later, Lue sent his mother a letter of apology and $500 for his betrothed who, according to custom, would not have been able to marry anyone else. But there was no reply, and his name was never restored.

Lue is, however, included in the official Burlingame genealogy as Fanny's adopted son. While Lue was in China, Fanny had joined her sister, Cynthia, and brother-in-law, William Dumville, in DeLand, Florida, where they owned five acres of orange groves. Wintering there eased Fanny's asthma and the symptoms of consumption that had surfaced shortly after Lue's departure. She arranged for him to join her.

For the next few years, he managed the orange grove and acted as manservant to Fanny's brother-in-law, who was sick with "creeping paralysis." After William's death in 1889, Lue and Fanny continued to winter in DeLand and summer in North Adams. He worked entirely in the groves, conducting citrus experiments and managing the additional property Fanny and Cynthia purchased.

Though Lue was supposed to be a part of the Burlingame family, his precise status was nebulous, even awkward. Lue acted more like a servant than an adopted son, passing out refreshments at parties and building fires at picnics. "While it did not make him one of them, he was among those present," one acute observer concluded.

Tolerated by the Burlingames' friends, Lue was held in scorn by Chinese in North Adams and nearby Boston; they dismissed him as a poor farmer living off missionary kindness. While it was true that Lue received no salary, he did work, and so long as Fanny was alive, he was secure, for no one doubted their mutual devotion. But when she died in 1903, he was cast adrift.

Fanny's sisters refused to acknowledge Lue's claim to Fanny's share of the Burlingame estate. In the wrangling that followed, Lue calculated his wages for seventeen years of service. The final settlement gave him $12,000 and Cynthia's and Fanny's property in DeLand. It was a bitter victory, however, as he had to agree never again to return to North Adams.

Cut off from both his adopted and birth families, Lue sought to create his own. Seven years before Fanny's death, she had hired a young Swedish woman, LaGette Hagstrom, as companion and personal maid. LaGette, a pretty, blue-eyed blonde, charmed all who met her, including Lue. When he returned to DeLand a man of property, he proposed marriage.

Whether LaGette refused him or her father denied permission is not known, but there was no marriage. Nevertheless, LaGette permitted Lue to deed his newly acquired property to her. This included the land the Burlingame sisters had deeded him and an additional piece he purchased for $4,000 shortly after his return from North Adams, 115 acres in all. Then, on December 4, 1906, the morning of her wedding to an old family friend, LaGette deeded the property back to Lue. She died unexpectedly seven months later.

Shy and diffident, Lue withdrew into himself. Instead of attending services at the First Baptist Church, he prayed alone in his grove. There were visitors, of course, neighbors and business acquaintances, but his only real companions were his two horses, which he called his children. Increasingly lonely, he threw himself into his work.

During his first winter in Florida, there had been a severe freeze, and Lue began experiments to develop an orange that would withstand sudden cold snaps. As described in the *Proceedings* of the American Pomological Society, Lue pollinated Harts Late with pollen from what was believed to be a Mediterranean Sweet tree.

LaGette Hagstrom's sisters and brothers and their friends were all welcome at Fanny Burlingame's, and they are pictured here with grove owners and northerners summering in DeLand. Lue Gim Gong is standing with the horses, Fanny is the elderly woman in the dark dress and cape, LaGette is third from the left in the front row, and the man she later married, Per Ekman, is first from the left in the back row. (Courtesy Ruth Hagstrom)

After Fanny's death, Lue no longer attended the services at the Baptist church. Instead he created a prayer garden in his grove. All visitors to Lue's grove were invited to this chapel, where he offered all-comprehensive, nonsectarian prayers for the good of his visitors, the country, and mankind, with a humble plea at the very end that God would help him to live for the good of others. Many people in DeLand today remember attending these services and also just stopping by to visit with Lue on his porch. (Courtesy Dr. Chih Meng)

Repeated falls from ladders while picking fruit and a series of accidents between 1904 and 1911 crippled Lue to the point where he needed crutches to walk. His horse— thirty-one and blind—followed him around the grove by listening for his whistle and then putting her nose to the ground to track his exact location. (Courtesy Him Mark Lai)

From the seeds that resulted, he raised twelve trees. Then he budded fifteen trees with this variety.

The oranges produced were good sized, full of juice, and hardy, enduring frosts with no apparent damage. The fruit was also capable of hanging on a tree through the rainy summer, allowing it to be held off the market until oranges were scarce and the highest price could be secured. Tests in 1909 proved the new orange's excellent shipping and keeping qualities, and growers hailed it as the year-round orange Florida needed to become competitive with the California citrus industry.

The prestigious Glen St. Mary Nurseries arranged to propagate and sell the finished trees. Lue's understanding was that he would receive a ten-cent royalty for each Lue Gim Gong tree *propagated* during the next four years. However, the written contract stipulated payment only for the trees *sold*. According to the nursery's sales brochure, "The contract price for the variety we believe far exceeds the price paid for any other orange or for any other fruit ever propagated in America." Lue claimed he received a mere $200, and he accused the nursery of deliberately holding off sales until the term of years expired.

Since Glen St. Mary Nurseries sold finished trees rather than budwood, a delay between the signing of the contract and the initial sales would have been unavoidable. The nursery might also have held up sales for marketing reasons. In the interim, testimonials from reputable growers were gathered and the Lue Gim Gong orange was submitted to the American Pomological Society for consideration for the distinguished Wilder Silver Medal, which it won in 1911, the same year the variety was finally marketed.

Controlling the budwood from which the trees were propagated was also difficult. As the nursery's proprietor, L. L. Taber, Jr., put it, "We did pretty well for about two years in controlling the Lue Gim Gong— after that it was a free-for-all," with people grafting other trees from stock purchased from Glen St. Mary Nurseries and even stealing grafts from Lue's grove. Though Lue lived up to his contract scrupulously— selling budwood only to the nursery—he unwittingly contributed to the problem by giving away budwood.

When well-known citrus grower William Chase Temple, impressed by the hardiness of the new orange, wanted to buy budwood for his own groves, Lue would not sell him a single bud. Instead, he offered to give him all he wanted for experimental purposes. Temple, not wanting to be under obligation, refused. While talking, he discovered that Lue had no Chinese ginger plants, so Temple sent him some from his own garden.

Selecting Ripe Oranges and Grapefruit in Lue Gim Gong's Citrus Groves, DeLand, Florida.

LUE GIM GONG'S CITRUS GROVES

Oranges, Grapefruit, Tangerines, Mandarins, Satsumas, Lemons, Etc. And the "Lue Gim Gong," An All Year-Round Orange and Grapefruit. Shipped From DeLand, Florida.

We spare no expense to make this fruit good. It is not picked from the trees indiscriminately, but is selected according to ripeness. Every orange is examined and wiped or brushed to remove dirt or other impurities, and they are carefully graded before sizing. The fruit in each box is of uniform size and wrapped in Hammerschlag waxed paper, such as is used for wrapping butter and candy. We have used this paper since 1889, and find that it tends to preserve the fruit and also to prevent those which are decayed from injuring any with which they may come in contact.

Our boxes are made by the W. A. Merryday Co., of Palatka, Fla., especially for us—are extra heavy and of the best quality and make.

No job or contract packing. This fruit not to be sold on condition but on its merits, and guaranteed to be good when received. As we would not wish to buy decayed fruit, neither do we sell it. "Therefore all things whatsoever ye would that men should do to you, do ye even so to them, for this is the law and the prophets." Matt. 7:12, and found in the teachings of Confucius. This is not my preaching but my practice in all things all my life. "Providing for honest things not only in the sight of the Lord but also in the sight of men." 2 Cor. 8:21. Faults I have, and mistakes I have made, but my intentions and aims are to be honest and honorable in all things or dealings and my will is good to encourage the right and discourage the wrong. If there are more honest and honorable and better ways to do business, even in my declining age, I am willing to learn. If any error address.

LUE GIM GONG
DeLand, Florida, or North Adams, Mass.

Lue's shipping label reveals his unique philosophy and manner of doing business. This picture of his grove was also sold as a postcard and printed on checks issued by banks in North Adams and DeLand. (Courtesy Dr. Chih Meng)

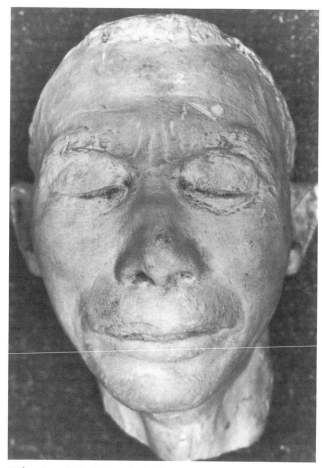

When Lue died, DeLand's leading citizens served as his pall-bearers, and a death mask was made in preparation for a full-sized monument of "this truly great Chinaman." Money for the statue was never raised, but a bust was completed and unveiled at the Florida Pavilion during the 1940 World's Fair in New York. (Courtesy Him Mark Lai)

Touched by his thoughtfulness, Lue asked the grower if he would accept a gift of Lue Gim Gong oranges as a token of his appreciation. When Temple said yes, Lue shipped him twelve oranges, each cut from the tree with a foot of precious budwood, enough to bud 100 branches.

As the number of Lue Gim Gong trees multiplied into the tens of thousands, Lue's fame spread. His belief that he had been wronged by Glen St. Mary Nurseries deepened, and when he developed the Gim Gong grapefruit (by crossing the common Florida grapefruit with the hardy perennial trifoliate orange), he refused to sell the rights, giving away the budwood instead.

The crop from Lue's grove, in its prime, should have generated an annual income of approximately $6,000, yet he could not meet his expenses. The thousands of visitors who came to see the "citrus wizard" each year always left with free samples. Also, while the industry in Florida was becoming more sophisticated, with growers marketing collectively through an exchange, Lue was mistrustful of relinquishing any control and refused to participate. And he was continually being cheated by unscrupulous independent distributors.

"Poor Lue defaulted 306 times by the American," he wrote the editor of the *Florida Grower*. "I not able stand no more. I must have the honest and honorable money to pay my bills. Helping poor solitary destitute Lue all alone in DeLand and in the world. God bless you all."

The editor published the letter in the January 31, 1917, issue, adding a plea of his own: "We are confronted with the lamentable fact that another American citizen has cheated the poor, helpless Chinaman, and I feel bitter humiliation that this should be a fact. I somehow feel a measure of guilt, of a sense of responsibility in this case; not so much as an individual as an American citizen."

Pointing out that the unpaid bill would be covered if 200 readers each contributed a dollar, the editor continued: "Let us give this meek and lowly man a square deal and make him realize that there is something more than mere words in the Christianity he has adopted from the white man. Do not delay, he needs the money and he needs it now. With Lue Gim Gong I say, 'God bless you.'"

Florida growers, though suffering losses from a freeze that winter, responded generously. Well over $200 was collected. It was not enough; Lue was forced to mortgage part, and then all, of his property.

Still experimenting, Lue developed many unusual plant combinations in his garden, including a rosebush that put forth seventeen different varieties in seven different colors, all from a single root. In 1921, the press widely reported his perfection of a unique, perfumed grapefruit. Twenty-one inches in circumference, the fruit resembled a shaddock. The sections were apparently too woody to eat, but a single grapefruit, when ripe, filled an entire room with its sweet, clean odor, and the skin could be made into a delectable crystallized candy and pickle. He also invented an all-purpose salve for treating a host of ailments including burns, skin diseases, mange, hemorrhoids, and nettle rash.

These creations did not bring Lue the money he needed, however, and his grove became so run-down that his crop in 1921 netted only $1,400. The entire proceeds had to be applied to the interest on his mortgages; when the loans came due, he could not pay them.

The *Florida Grower* again came to his rescue with a scheme to raise $6,000 through $100 bonds. The De-Land and North Adams newspapers also took up the cause. S. M. Moore, of the Tampa West Coast Realty Company, spoke for many when he wrote: "If the men who are interested in the citrus industry of this state, even in a small way, would consider just for a minute what a benefit this fine old man has been to the industry, surely everyone would subscribe $100 or more to this fund. While it is an investment, with good security, it is also a debt we owe Lue Gim Gong. Let's don't fail to get up the entire amount necessary."

Donations—prompted by admiration, respect, and pity—trickled in from growers, strangers who had visited the grove, people who had known Lue in happier days in North Adams. The money saved his home and provided financial security for his few remaining years. But he had to wait for death—on June 3, 1925—to release him from the loneliness he had endured since Mother Fanny's death.

Mary and Joseph Tape
(Dates of birth and death not known)
From China to San Francisco, California
(Portrait reconstructed by Tang You Shan from an 1892 woodcut)

Mary and Joseph Tape
and Their Fight for Education

In 1884, Mary and Joseph Tape created a statewide sensation when they attempted to enroll their eight-year-old daughter, Mamie, in a San Francisco public school and refused to take *no* for an answer.

The battle lines in the Tapes' fight for an education for Mamie and all Chinese children had been drawn long before. As early as 1852, the Chinese in San Francisco had declared in a public letter: "If the privileges of your laws are open to us, some of us will doubtless acquire your language, your ideas, your feelings, your morals, your forms and become citizens of your country." But the response of white San Franciscans was reflected in a typical *Daily Alta California* editorial: "[Chinese] are not of that kind that Americans can ever associate or sympathize with. They are not of our people and never will be, though they remain here forever."

Petitions from Chinese for admission into the city's schools were therefore consistently denied until 1859, when the San Francisco Board of Education, bowing to pressure from the Chinese community and its advocates, grudgingly permitted Chinese into the evening school's foreign classes. It also accepted a long-standing proposal by the Reverend William Speer, a former Presbyterian missionary to China, to open a public day school for Chinese children in his church.

The teacher's salary of seventy-five dollars a month was the taxpayers' only expense. Nevertheless, the Board repeatedly closed the school due to lack of funds. For seven years, Chinese, insisting on their right to school privileges as taxpayers, were able to force the Board to reopen the school each time. But the rise of anti-Chinese sentiment in the late 1860s eventually led to the school's permanent closure and to the withdrawal of Chinese from public-supported evening classes.

From 1871 to 1885, the only education available to Chinese in San Francisco was through church-sponsored classes and schools. The first Sabbath and evening school had been started in 1854 by the Reverend Speer, who realized that Chinese needed to learn English before they could understand the Gospel. Chinese immigrants who worked during the day flocked to the school, which taught English and other subjects in addition to religion. Other churches began similar evening classes and Sunday schools.

It is likely that Joseph Tape learned his English in a Sunday school. Only thirteen when he emigrated, he had adopted American dress and manners and cut his queue. His English was so fluent that in addition to working as an expressman and drayman, he interpreted for the Imperial Chinese Consulate. His wife, Mary, had been eleven when missionaries returning from Shanghai took her with them to San Francisco. Brought up by the Ladies Relief Society, she spoke excellent English and very little Chinese.

The church-sponsored schools were not convenient for the Tapes' children, however, as the family did not live in Chinatown, where these schools were located. When Joseph tried to enroll Mamie in their neighborhood school, the San Francisco School Board denied his application.

The Board's decision was backed by the State Education Code, which gave school trustees "the power to exclude children of filthy or vicious habits, or children with contagious or infectious diseases." To members of the San Francisco Board of Education, all Chinese children, including Mamie, fell into one or all of these categories. They therefore rejected Joseph's application just as they had rejected those of the many Chinese parents before him.

A few days after the Board's refusal to admit Mamie to Spring Valley School, the Chinese Consul, F. A. Bee, wrote San Francisco School Superintendent Andrew Jackson Moulder: "The reasons given by you, if correctly reported through the press, are so inconsistent with the treaties, Constitution, and laws of the United States, especially so in this case as the child is native born, that I consider it my duty to renew the request to admit the child, and all other Chinese children resident here who desire to enter the public schools under your charge."

Moulder, supported by the State Superintendent of Education, stood firm. At its October 21, 1884, meeting, the San Francisco Board of Education adopted a resolution on a vote of eight to three that any principal or teacher who admitted "a Mongolian child" would be subject to immediate dismissal. Three weeks later, Spring Valley School Principal Jennie Hurley, Superintendent Moulder, and the San Francisco Board of Education were summoned to appear before Superior Court Judge James G. Maguire to show cause why the daughter of Joseph Tape should not be allowed to enter the public schools.

Sunday schools for the Chinese, often the only schools available to them, could be found in more than seventy cities including Boston, Philadelphia, New York, Chicago, Pittsburgh, and New Orleans. Regardless of where the schools were located, the idea behind them was to teach the Chinese enough English so they could understand the gospel, convert, and then return to China as missionaries. Students often showed their gratitude to their teachers with gifts and banquets, and the Chinese students at the Baptist and Presbyterian churches in New York City organized the picnic illustrated here. Held at Iona Island, the event included swimming, kite flying, boating, football, music, fireworks, and plenty of food. Of the 300 persons invited, however, fewer than half attended, as many of the teachers did not want to socialize with the Chinese, only to "save their souls." (Courtesy Wong Chin Foo Collection)

What encouraged the Chinese to turn Joseph's request for Mamie's admission into a test case was an 1884 decision by the United States Circuit Court for the Ninth Judicial District to allow Look Tin Sing, a Chinese boy born in Mendocino County, California, to disembark in the United States after a five-year visit to China. He had been refused entry by San Francisco immigration officials on the grounds that his admission would be a violation of the 1882 Exclusion Act. The court disagreed, ruling that "birth within the dominions of the United States of itself creates citizenship and that every person born within those dominions, whatever the status of his parents, is a natural-born citizen" and should be treated as such. Since Mamie was "a natural-born citizen," it stood to reason that she should be entitled to the free education that was every American's birthright.

Judge Maguire agreed. In his decision on January 9, 1885, he stated:

> To deny a child, born of Chinese parents in this State, entrance to the public schools would be a violation of the law of the State and the Constitution of the United States. It would, moreover, be unjust to levy a forced tax upon Chinese residents to help maintain our schools, and yet prohibit their children born here from education in those schools. . . . The Board of Education have ample power to keep out all children who are blighted by filth, infection or contagion, or who are daily brought in contact with population of any kind. But any such objection should be personal to each particular child so barred out, without regard to its race or color. In the case at bar, it is admitted that the child is healthy and of cleanly habits, and of healthy and cleanly surroundings, and her application for admission as a pupil in the Spring Valley School is proper and lawful and must be granted.

While the Board appealed the decision, Mamie remained out of school. On March 3, 1885, the California Supreme Court confirmed Judge Maguire's decision. Superintendent Moulder's response was to persuade the State Legislature to modify the school code yet again, and quickly, so that any Chinese students the court forced the schools to accept would at least be segregated from white children.

The San Francisco Board of Education was reluctant to make *any* concessions to the Chinese, however. Still hoping to refuse them an education entirely, the members dragged their feet in establishing a Chinese school.

Public schools in California's small rural towns were sometimes integrated despite the state code. In 1917, Florence Ruth Tom (front), who had previously been tutored at home, enrolled in the first integrated class in Colusa High School. Going to public school meant children from Chinatown had to cross the railroad tracks into "white territory," and Florence and her young foster brother were taunted daily by white boys who shouted "Chink" and "Chinaman" at them. Finally, Florence decided to teach the boys a lesson by egging them on until they crossed the tracks into "Chinese territory," where she beat them soundly. She and her foster brother were not annoyed again. (Courtesy Theodore Tang)

Ning Huie and his wife, Lin-Shee—farmers in Walla Walla,
Washington, and Lewiston, Idaho—solved the problem of
their children's education by hiring a governess, Mrs. Mocho.
(Courtesy Christine Richardson)

So little Mamie Tape, flanked by her two attorneys, returned to Spring Valley School on April 7, 1885, and asked Principal Hurley to admit her in accordance with the decision of the Supreme Court.

The request was made in a writ of mandate directed to Hurley and issued by Judge Lawler. Principal Hurley, supported by the presence of the Superintendent and other school officials, refused to admit Mamie on the grounds that the child did not have the vaccination certificate required by the Board. When Mamie's attorneys argued that the writ superseded any Board ruling, Hurley put them off by claiming the classes were full and agreeing to register Mamie and place her on a waiting list.

Furious over her child's public humiliation, Mary Tape wrote a lengthy letter of protest to the Board of Education:

I see that you are going to make all sorts of excuses to keep my child out off the Public Schools. Dear Sirs, Will you please tell me! Is it a disgrace to be born a Chinese? Didn't God make us all!!! What right! have you to bar my children out of the school because she is a chinese Descend. They is no other worldly reason that you could keep her out, except that I suppose, you all goes to churches on Sundays! Do you call that a Christian act. . . . You have expended a lot of the Public money foolishly, all because of one poor little Child. . . . It seems no matter how a Chinese may live and dress so long as you know they Chinese then they are hated as one. There is not any right or justice for them. [mistakes in original]

Dated April 8, 1885, Mary's letter was read before the Board on April 15. By then the Board—realizing that it would either have to admit Mamie and other Chinese children into the public schools with white children or establish a segregated school—had rented rooms above a grocery store in Chinatown for the Chinese Primary School. Though Mary had sworn, "Mamie Tape will never attend any of the Chinese schools of your making! Never!!!" Mamie and her younger brother, Frank, were the first two students to appear when the school opened on April 13. They really had little choice, for it would take decades of petitions and appeals by the Chinese community before their children could attend integrated schools.

The local press reported in detail the opening of the Chinese Primary School, and there were so many visitors that the teacher had to set aside Friday afternoons to accommodate them. When the spectators found clean, well-behaved children wearing Western clothes and fluently speaking, reading, and writing English, their curiosity faded and the Tapes disappeared from the newspapers until August 4, 1889.

Their reappearance in the news had nothing to do with the school issue but with Mary's talents and achievements. The article, "Our Chinese Edison," was actually about Wong Hong Tai's experiments and achievements with photography and electrical science. According to Tai, "A good many Chinese take a great interest in telegraphy and the telephone, but nearly all are too busy to prosecute their studies beyond acquiring the Morse alphabet and making themselves fairly expert in sending and receiving social messages."

The one exception he noted was Mary Tape, whom he deemed his equal in both telegraphy and photography, and with whom he spent a great deal of time on the telephone "discussing science at long range." With the goal of photographing "trotters in motion and birds in their flight," Mary was then creating extra-sensitive dry plates to keep up with a new camera Tai was inventing.

A subsequent article in the November 3, 1892, *Morning Call* detailed Mary's achievements as a self-taught photographer, artist, and telegrapher, and as a mother of four musically accomplished children. Again there was no mention of the Tapes' fight to secure public education for their children. As described by the reporter, the Tape home was an extraordinarily happy one, and Joseph's only regret was that although he had adopted the United States as his home, he could not vote.

When asked if they would go to China, Mary replied, "We may go some day if we feel that we can afford the trip, but it will only be as tourists visiting a foreign country. California is our home. All of our best and happiest moments have been passed here, and here we shall live and die."

Chin Gee-hee 1844–1930
From Luk Chuen Village, China, to Seattle, Washington (Courtesy
International Examiner)

Chin Gee-hee, Railroad Baron

The day that changed Chin Gee-hee's life began inauspiciously. The villages around Luk Chuen in Toishan rotated their market days, and that morning, as he had done every morning for as long as he could remember, Gee-hee rose before the rooster and bundled the soy sauce crocks his father made into two nets, tying one onto each end of his carrying pole. Stooping, he hoisted the pole across his shoulders and set out for the market.

The load was not heavy but it was fragile. Gee-hee, knowing what the loss of even one jar would mean to a family as poor as his, stepped warily along the muddy path that separated the fields. Nearer the market, the path widened and his pace quickened as he joined the stream of farmers and peddlers.

Nearby, a group of boys only a little younger than Gee-hee kicked a shuttlecock. The game, mild at first, intensified. Suddenly the shuttlecock landed in front of Gee-hee. Heedless of anything beyond their game, the boys dove for it, knocking Gee-hee and those nearest him onto the ground. For a few minutes, curses, squeals, and squawks flew as fast as feathers and fists. Scrambling out from under pigs, chickens, men and boys, Gee-hee surveyed the mess: every one of his father's crocks was shattered. Quietly, he began to pick up the pieces.

An old man, known only as Uncle Hung, watched. He did not have to know Gee-hee to understand the enormity of the boy's loss. Families in Toishan—reduced to starvation by ungiving Gods, greedy officials and landlords, bandits, and interdialectical feuds—had been sending fathers, husbands, and sons overseas to work under conditions so terrible that the trade in their labor was commonly called the selling of piglets. Uncle Hung had been a piglet. But unlike those who had died in the holds of ships or on plantations in the colonies of the New World, Uncle Hung had found wealth in America. He had not made enough to retire, however, and now, impressed by Gee-hee's calm in the face of calamity, he invited the boy to join him when he returned to America, the country Chinese called Gold Mountain.

Nothing more is known about Uncle Hung or when the old man and boy set out for America. But by 1862, Gee-hee, then eighteen years old, was working in Port Gamble, Washington. While the majority of Chinese in the area were chasing dreams of gold through placer mining, Gee-hee worked as a laborer, launderer, and then cook at the Port Gamble lumber mill, saving enough money to send for a wife. Their son, born in 1875, is believed to have been the first Chinese baby born in the Northwest; a few years later, a daughter was born.

In 1873, Gee-hee, now conversant in English, moved to Seattle, where he became a junior partner in the Wah Chong Company, a multi-functional enterprise that manufactured cigars, did tailoring, and acted as a retail and wholesale outlet for tea and other goods from China and as an exporter of flour and other northwestern products to Asia. It also advertised the availability of Chinese help "on short notice." It was this aspect of the business that had attracted Gee-hee.

Developing the rich resources of the Pacific Northwest and building a transportation network to give access to these resources required vast pools of labor, labor for which Gee-hee intended to become a conduit. Traveling throughout the region, he acquired labor contracts from lumber camps, coal mines, railroad companies, farms, and canneries. He then recruited men from the boatloads arriving on the regular run from China to Seattle, and from among Chinese already in America.

Generally, a gang of forty men (including at least one cook and a bilingual "boss") was contracted for at a fixed price and number of months. As the broker, Gee-hee was responsible for paying the laborers, after taking out a percentage for himself. More profit came from his company's sale of supplies to the men.

Like other Chinese merchant enterprises, the Wah Chong Company became a center for Chinese laborers, providing sleeping quarters and eating facilities, letter-writing and translation services, a mailing address, a bank, and a place to share news and exchange gossip. Merchants, near the bottom of the social strata in China, rose to the top in America. It was therefore Gee-hee who took command when trouble came.

Washington Territory had never welcomed the Chinese. But when cheap labor was required to fill swamps, dig tunnels, and build bridges, the lack of white men willing to do the work was so obvious that even the most ardent anti-Chinese could not protest. From the

A few laborers who knew English became labor contractors. Ah Quin, a successful labor contractor for the Southern California Railroad, learned English at a Christian missionary school in Canton before emigrating to the United States in 1868. Literate in Chinese and English, he maintained a diary in both languages that provides rare insights into the difficulties of recruiting men and managing the logistics of supplies. (Courtesy San Diego Historical Society)

1860s to the early 1880s, Chinese (many of them under contract to Gee-hee) worked on railroad construction projects and in the Newcastle, Coal Creek, and Renton coal mines. These jobs, rejected by whites during boom times, became coveted prizes during the drastic economic depression that hit the Pacific Northwest between 1883 and 1886.

Under the Exclusion Act passed by Congress in 1882, Chinese laborers were no longer permitted to land in America. Out-of-work whites (many of them also immigrants) wanted Chinese already in America to leave as well. The cry "The Chinese must go!" reverberated throughout the Territory in newspapers, rallies, and torchlight processions. Anger exploded into scattered incidents of violence. Then, at a mass rally in Seattle on September 28, 1885, delegates from Tacoma, Puyallup, Sumner, Olympia, and other Puget Sound cities agreed to expel all Chinese from the Territory by November 1.

The Committee of Fifteen, which included a judge, lawyers, businessmen, and contractors, was charged with carrying out the program of expulsion in Tacoma. The Committee posted unsigned notices in Chinatown ordering the Chinese to leave, and it urged all employers to dismiss their Chinese employees immediately, persuading the reluctant with threats of violence against them and their families.

When the Reverend W. D. McFarland denounced these tactics in a fiery sermon, a number of his parishioners walked out of the church. "Go!" he shouted after them. "Go! I will preach on till the benches are empty."

Seven other pastors banded with him in defense of the Chinese. In a joint statement issued on October 26, they warned: "Liberty for ourselves, established upon despotism over others, will be dearly bought. Indeed, liberty is threatened with death when any class of men are stripped with impunity of their legal rights."

For vengeance, the Committee posted the pastors' names and those of other sympathizers. Nevertheless, a few stood their ground. When a mob demanded that Mrs. Bowen "put out" her Chinese servant, she yelled back, "Put him out nothing!" and charged at them with her broom. Another woman, similarly outraged, brandished a shotgun.

By the end of October, Tacoma's Chinese population had shrunk from 800 to 200. The majority of laborers, unable to find employment and afraid for their lives, had left for Portland and Vancouver. But merchants, unable to dispose of their goods, remained.

Finally, on the morning of November 3, hundreds of white men armed with clubs and pistols marched into Chinatown, kicking in doors. According to one mer-

Labor contractors like Ah Quin and Chin Gee-hee were able to build financial empires and enjoy family life. But the Exclusion laws forced most laborers to live as lonely "bachelors." Despite frugality that often bordered on deprivation, a large number of laborers, such as these three Central Pacific Railroad workers, were unable to ever save enough from their wages to rejoin their families in China. (Courtesy Amon Carter Museum)

Thirty years after the expulsion of Chinese from Tacoma, Judge James Wickersham, one of the Committee of Fifteen, insisted, "I have always felt that we did a great and good work for the Pacific Coast that day. If given an equal chance with our people, {Chinese} would outdo {us} in the struggle for life and gain possession of the Pacific Coast of America. . . . We cannot compete with them, not because of their baser qualities, but because of their better." (Courtesy Washington State Historical Society)

chant, Mow Lung, the mob included the mayor. "They took hold of the Chinese that were in these houses, some of whom were Chinese women, including my wife, and pulled them out [into the street]."

Another merchant, Lum May, told how his wife was dragged out of their house when she refused to leave. "From the excitement, the fright, and the losses we sustained through the riot she lost her reason. She was hopelessly insane and attacked people with a hatchet or any other weapon if not watched."

The Chinese, surrounded by armed white men on horseback, trudged in driving rain through eight miles of mud to the railroad station. Shivering from cold, wet, and fear, they bought tickets for Portland. Those who could not pay the fare were loaded into the boxcars of a southbound freight. A few walked south along the tracks they had helped to build. The rest huddled together under blankets brought by a few sympathetic whites and the handful of Chinese merchants who had been granted an additional two days' grace. By the time the passenger train arrived, two men had died of exposure. The rest boarded the train, taking the bodies with them. Their homes and businesses were burned to the ground later in the day.

Seattle's own Committee of Fifteen had also served notice to the Chinese to leave by November 1. As in

Tacoma, many of the laborers did leave, but Gee-hee and other merchants remained to collect on their accounts, settle their affairs, and attempt to gain reimbursement for their property. Chinese laborers, driven out of other towns, poured in, and though most companies were replacing Chinese workers with whites, blacks, and Native Americans, Wah Chong continued to advertise "contract labor on short notice."

As soon as the news from Tacoma reached Seattle, however, Gee-hee wired the Chinese Consul in San Francisco for help:

Chinese residents of Tacoma forcibly driven out yesterday, from two to three hundred Chinese now in Seattle. Imminent danger. Local authorities willing but not strong enough to protect us. We ask you to secure protection for us.
Chin Gee-hee for Wah Chong Company

Mayor Henry Yesler wired Governor Squire for troops. The Governor immediately passed the request on to the United States Secretary of the Interior and issued a proclamation appealing to the people in the Territory to maintain law and order. Though the Secretary admonished Squire to protect the Chinese with available forces, he did not see the necessity for sending

Individual acts of defiance by whites on behalf of Chinese were not unusual. In 1908, when Wong Kee went to Rhyolite, Nevada, to settle some business, he was not allowed to eat in the restaurant, so Walter Scott bought lunch for them both and sat down in the middle of the street to eat with him. (Courtesy Chinese Culture Foundation Collection, Asian American Studies Library, University of California at Berkeley)

federal troops. But the Consul General's reply assured Gee-hee:

> We are doing everything possible. Think Kowoon Bing [National Guard] will be sent today.
> Ow-yang Ming, Consul General

On the morning of November 5, Gee-hee met with Mayor Yesler, representatives of the Committee of Fifteen, law and order advocates, and others. Gee-hee and the Mayor had been friends for almost twenty years. In fact, it had been Yesler who had encouraged Gee-hee to move from Port Gamble to Seattle. While building Wah Chong into the largest labor contractor in the Puget Sound area, Gee-hee had become friendly with many other influential citizens, including Thomas Burke, the legal counsel for the white working men.

That night, at a mass meeting of all Seattle citizens called by Mayor Yesler, Thomas Burke attacked the Mayor of Tacoma: "[J. Robert Weisbach] is a foreigner and can hardly speak the English language. I have read how Germans rose up against the Jews and drove them from their homes. I remember how they drove the Russian peasants out; but what am I to think when only thirty miles from where I stand, in the Republic of the United States, such atrocities have been committed. It could not be done under an American. It was done under a German." His words inflamed the crowd and he was booed as a "white Chinaman." But the Chinese later erected a statue of Burke in appreciation of his support.

On November 7, President Cleveland issued a Proclamation of Martial Law and ordered ten companies of the Nineteenth Infantry to Seattle from Fort Vancouver. While the 350 federal troops did maintain overall order, one group of soldiers took advantage of the situation and collected a "special tax" from the citizens of Chinatown, netting about $150. Some even attacked the very people they were supposed to be protecting: four Chinese were beaten up in unprovoked assaults, one had his queue cut off, one was thrown down a flight of stairs, and another was hurled into the bay.

Many Chinese fled to Portland despite a wire from the Consul General to Gee-hee urging them to remain in Washington Territory. Seattle, however, remained quiet; the troops left, and emigration slowed to a trickle.

Though the next two months passed in relative calm, ultimate expulsion was inevitable. On the morning of February 7, 1886, Gee-hee, his family, and approximately 350 remaining Chinese were rounded up at

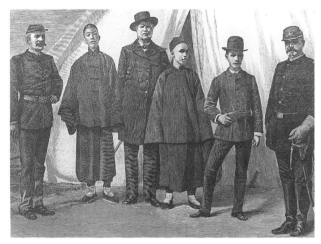

One of the worst massacres of Chinese in America occurred in Rock Springs, Wyoming, in 1885, when violence exploded between white and Chinese coal miners. In the riot that followed, Chinatown was gutted by fire. Chinese who hid smothered or burned; those who fled were shot. Others, escaping into the hills bareheaded and barefooted, died from exposure and hunger or were killed and eaten by wolves. In all, twenty-eight died. Representatives of the Chinese government and United States military officers arrived to investigate and to protect returning Chinese. (Courtesy Philip Choy)

Slowly, relations between Chinese and whites improved. By World War I, descendants of the Chinese survivors fought side by side in France with descendants of the rioters. And in the 1920s, the local unions of the United Mine Workers of America honored miners retiring to China, including these four, with banquets. (Courtesy Wyoming State Archives, Museums and Historical Department)

Chinese pioneer men frequently found themselves in their forties before they saved enough to marry and raise a family. Ah Louis (top left), a labor contractor and entrepreneur in San Luis Obispo, California, emigrated to the Oregon gold fields in 1856 as a young man of eighteen. But he was forty-one when he married Gon Ying (top right), a woman of nineteen from San Francisco, who gave him five sons and three daughters before dying of pneumonia in 1909. "Dad was very progressive," his son Howard recalled. "{The Ah Louis Store} was the very first to have electricity. People would come from miles around in their buggies just to wait for us to turn on the lights."

Ah Louis allowed his children considerable freedom, raising no objections when his daughter Helen, a pianist, traveled 200 miles and more on weekends to play with an all-male band she joined while still in high school. Moving to Chicago after graduation from California Polytechnic Institute, Helen played with various bands (left) and toured in vaudeville (right). (Courtesy Howard Louis and Helen Wong Jean)

dawn and forced to march to the waterfront. One hundred ninety-six of them, as many as the Captain would allow, were loaded onto the *Queen of the Pacific*. The rest, including Gee-hee and his family, were herded into a warehouse and kept under protection by the Home Guard, which the Sheriff and Mayor had hastily summoned by ringing the city's church bells.

Since the next steamer for San Francisco was not due until February 14, the Sheriff was reluctant to keep the Chinese confined in the warehouse, and the decision was made to escort them back to their quarters. A roadblock soon stopped them. In the riot that followed, Gee-hee tried to keep the Chinese together, but it was impossible. At one point Gee-hee and his family were captured by the mob and then rescued by the Home Guard. Amazingly, neither they nor any of the other Chinese were injured.

Seven days later, 110 Chinese boarded the *George W. Elder,* while others were sent to Port Townsend to board another ship. Only Gee-hee's family and a few others were able to remain in Seattle under the protection of

Mayor Yesler, Thomas Burke, and other prominent and sympathetic citizens.

With legal advice from Burke, Gee-hee devoted the next several months to recording the damage done by mobs to Chinese businesses and homes. He then forwarded his detailed account and list of damages to the Chinese legation. After years of negotiation, the final compensation for property lost was over $700,000.

By then, Chinese were slowly drifting back to Seattle, their presence tolerated because the Territory was lobbying for statehood, which was granted in 1889. That same year a devastating fire destroyed much of Seattle, and workers were once again in demand for rebuilding and filling the labor needs of new enterprises that were beginning to emerge. Because of the Exclusion Act, Gee-hee could not find enough Chinese to fill the contracts and he brought in Japanese workers from Portland.

In 1888, Gee-hee had opened his own business, the Quong Tuck Company, which sold general merchandise and imports from China, though its primary business

Chin Gee-hee erected the first new brick building in Seattle after the 1889 fire. His company, Quong Tuck, occupied one of the two storefronts, and it was in this office that he conceived the idea for the Sun Ning Railroad in Toishan. (Courtesy Special Collections Division, University of Washington Libraries)

The Sun Ning Railroad, torn apart in the 1930s to hinder invading Japanese troops, was never rebuilt. A statue of Chin Gee-hee was later erected in a small park near the former station, now a bus terminus. (Courtesy Lily Song. Photograph by Ou Guo Lou)

was labor contracting. Gee-hee therefore not only provided the masons for constructing the Burke Building (which occupied an entire city block), but he also helped Thomas Burke, now a judge, furnish his new offices with beautiful screens and other furnishings imported from China.

But it was the railroad that truly captured Gee-hee's imagination. From track laborer he had become a contractor and then a general agent. Judge Burke and J. J. Hill of the Great Northern Railroad arranged for him to tour some of the principal railway lines, and Gee-hee dreamed of building a railroad in his native district of Toishan.

The majority of nineteenth century Chinese emigrants were from Toishan. Most of them sent money home, and their remittances changed the county from one of the poorest in southern China to one of the richest. But as Gee-hee observed on his periodic visits home, transportation had not changed since his boyhood—people had the choice of walking or, if they had the money, riding in sedan chairs, while commodities were carried in handcarts.

Having taken an active part in developing an effective transportation system for the state of Washington, Gee-hee understood that a similar system was crucial for the development of China. He was determined to build a railroad that would facilitate the transportation of people and necessities in Toishan.

The people in Toishan were enthusiastic. Since successful emigrants often contributed money for building schools, orphanages, and hospitals at home, Gee-hee believed they would subscribe for a railroad. In 1904 he turned his business over to his son and son-in-law. Then, together with a fellow Toishanese, Yu Shek, he formed the Sun Ning Railway Company. They divided the task of fund-raising. While Vice President Yu Shek solicited money from overseas Chinese in Southeast Asia, President Chin Gee-hee traveled to Chinese communities in cities all across North America.

Sun Ning Railway Company shares sold for five yuan or $2.50. Through news stories, advertisements, and frequent public lectures, Gee-hee and Yu Shek raised $1.4 million in a single year from Chinese in America, Canada, Australia, Singapore, Hong Kong, and Toishan. Many of the investors were laborers, some were merchants; individual investments ranged from a few to one thousand shares.

Raising the money proved easier than building the railroad. To gain access to China's bureaucracy and to rally support from the gentry, Gee-hee had to buy a title. Even then the company was repeatedly forced to change its planned routes because of local objections. It took fourteen years—from May 1906 to March 1920—and $4.8 million to construct 137 kilometers of railway.

During construction, Gee-hee returned to Seattle several times to raise additional monies. He also contracted with Richard Schellens in Seattle to purchase all the necessary rails, ties, plates, and rolling stock for the railroad. When construction was finally completed, Judge Thomas Burke said, "Seattle can point to no business career of higher honor, and few of more value to it, than that of Chin Gee-hee," and he was made an honorary member of the Seattle Chamber of Commerce. Only two other men had ever been thus honored.

As Gee-hee had anticipated, the effect of modern transportation on Toishan was tremendous. Three million passengers and 100,000 tons of cargo were transported annually. All the towns along the railroad prospered. The railroad also promoted the growth of modern industries, the development of river navigation lines, and the creation of a highway bureau in 1920.

A visionary with regard to transportation, Gee-hee was a staunch traditionalist in his family life. During his periodic visits home, he acquired a total of six wives. When the wife of his American-born son failed to produce a male child, Gee-hee forced his son to abandon her and their eleven-year-old daughter, Margaret. According to Margaret, her grandfather was prepared to have her and her mother killed, and they barely escaped with their lives.

The last decade of Gee-hee's own life was fraught with difficulties as he and the government struggled over control of the railroad. Yet his letters to his good friend Judge Burke were full of plans to expand the railroad so it would be possible to "take train [at Sun Ning] and rail the whole way to points in Europe." He also wanted to open a free port that would "enable the Chinese people [abroad] to ship to China direct without having to have all cargoes first land on British soil." Sounding more like a young man than an octagenarian, he wrote, "I am so full of this port business that I scarcely eat or sleep."

These new dreams were not realized, however, before his death in 1929. The Sun Ning Railroad was dismantled in the late 1930s to deter invading Japanese military forces. It was never rebuilt.

Ing Hay 1862–1952
*From Hsai Pin Li Village, China, to John Day, Oregon
(Courtesy Oregon Historical Society)*

Lung On 1863–1940
*From Sun Wui, China, to John Day, Oregon (Courtesy
Oregon Historical Society)*

Ing Hay, Healer,
and Lung On, Entrepreneur

The woman shifted nervously in the hard wooden chair. Ing Hay, popularly known as "Doc" Hay, had been highly recommended. But she felt strange going to a doctor in a general store rather than a proper office; and the slight Chinese man taking her pulse had asked no questions, merely told her in heavily accented English to sit, then lightly grasped her wrist.

His fingers moved from one pulse point to another. "You have five children."

The woman, startled, shook her head no. "Four," she told him. "I have four."

Raising five fingers for emphasis, Doc Hay insisted, "Five."

"Oh, yes," the woman agreed, remembering. "But one didn't live."

It was not the first time Doc Hay had surprised a patient. Once, he had told a war veteran suffering from a stiff neck that the problem was due to shell splinters embedded in the man's neck, and X-rays at a hospital had substantiated his diagnosis. His herbs and liniments had cured a girl of polio. And he successfully treated stomach ulcers, kidney ailments, rheumatism, blood poisoning, meningitis, influenza, hemorrhaging, lumbago, and rattlesnake bites.

To his non-Chinese patients, Doc Hay's skills seemed magical. But his Chinese patients were familiar with the tradition of pulse diagnosis that Hay practiced. According to this system of medicine, there are twenty-eight qualities of pulse that can be used to assess a patient's medical history and forecast the probable course of an illness. Doc Hay, coming from a long line of skilled herbalists in Toishan, was a skilled diagnostician.

In the early 1880s, poverty had driven Hay and his father to Walla Walla, Washington, in search of gold. By the time the two arrived, however, most of the gold was gone. Within two years, Hay's father returned home as poor as when he had left. He had wanted his son to go with him, but Hay persuaded his father to let him try his luck in John Day, Oregon, where other kinsmen had settled.

The all-male Chinese community of John Day (about 600) centered around Kam Wah Chung & Co., a grocery store and hiring hall for Chinese laborers. Though gold in the area was played out, ranches, farms, and logging camps needed carpenters, cooks, and cowboys, all of whom were available through the store's proprietor, Lung On.

While Hay was never able to master English, Lung On—better known as Leon—was fluent. He enjoyed reading Charles Dickens and Guy de Maupassant, and his penmanship was so beautiful that a merchant with whom Leon did business framed and hung one of his orders.

Hay and Leon, both in their early twenties, were different in other ways. Hay was quiet and religious. Leon, born to wealth and trained as a Confucian scholar in his native Sunwui, was outgoing, a gambler, and a womanizer. But in 1886, when Leon invited Hay to become his partner in Kam Wah Chung & Co., Hay agreed. Their partnership endured for over half a century, ending only through death.

Because of Leon, Doc Hay was able to extend his herbal practice beyond the immediate community of John Day. For fear of damaging his hands, Hay would never handle anything rough—even coarse paper—and he often wore a glove to protect the hand he used for diagnosis. It was therefore Leon who drove him to outlying farms and ranches, first by horse and buggy and then by automobile.

Hay often took over patients that doctors of Western medicine had failed to cure. One former patient, Lillian Davis, recalled, "In 1905 I was twelve years old and came down with inflammatory rheumatism. Dr. J. H. Fell, the only American doctor in John Day, told my father that if I lived I would always be a cripple. Dr. Hay with his cooked herbs . . . dispelled all effects of the ailment."

That same year, Hay was charged by doctors of Western medicine in Grant County with practicing medicine illegally. One pioneer correctly predicted that "no jury would convict him"; instead, his reputation spread as Leon wrote and sent out advertisements describing Hay's successes.

Leon translated for Hay, handled the correspondence, and packed the necessary medicines for patients all over Oregon and Washington. An astute businessman, he also expanded Kam Wah Chung & Co., selling supplies and imported goods to non-Chinese.

In frontier towns, fire prevention was critical, and one of the Fourth of July contests in Deadwood, South Dakota, was the great Hub-and-Hub Race between the hose teams. In 1888, the winning team was Chinatown's. (Courtesy South Dakota State Historical Society)

The practice of medicine in frontier towns was often a matter of luck. It was not uncommon for non-Chinese to seek medical help from traditional Chinese doctors, who frequently advertised their services in newspapers. One advertisement in El Paso, Texas, suggested, "When your case has been given up as hopeless by others, give us a trial." Another, in Denver, Colorado, offered medical advice by mail. Lee Me Him (left) practiced in Wyoming. (Courtesy Wyoming State Archives, Museums and Historical Department)

Chinese had settled around the store after nearby Canyon City's Chinatown was destroyed by fire in 1885 and local authorities would not allow them to rebuild. For the most part, Chinese and non-Chinese in John Day coexisted peaceably. Leon and his buckaroo friend Markee Tom (both affectionately dubbed "Oriental Barbarians") rode with white buckaroos and even dated white women without incident. But an advertisement placed by Kam Wah Chung & Co. and two other Chinese businesses in the January 3, 1902, issue of the *Blue Mountain Eagle* warned that those who "conducted themselves in an unlawful manner" in Chinatown would be prosecuted "to the extent of the law," indicating that there were at least occasional problems.

Then, on April 17, 1905, a mob of white men broke into the Kam Wah Chung building. They arrested Leon and two other Chinese and ransacked the store, taking some of Doc Hay's herbs, a small quantity of opium, and a few opium pipes. Opium was widely used in patent medicines of the period, and Kam Wah Chung & Co. purchased its supply from an American wholesaler, the Spokane Drug Company, in Washington. Leon pleaded not guilty and was acquitted in a jury trial.

The charges against Leon and Doc Hay were probably the result of jealousy over their success. Under Leon's management, the store and Hay's practice flourished. Leon invested their profits in property and shares in dairies and gold mines. The store was the first business in the area to install a telephone and electricity, and Leon started the first automobile dealership east of the Cascades.

Yet Hay never sent money home. His family in China included a wife, son, and daughter as well as parents, all of them desperately poor. "The moaning of your family from the cold and crying from hunger can be heard frequently," a cousin wrote Hay. "This spring I lent them some money when I found they were going to stretch their hands to beg from door to door. Since our great-grandfather, no one in our family has been reduced to such barefaced shame as to beg. [But] that small amount of money borrowed from me must have been used up. If you do not send money back, they will probably have to embark upon the road of begging."

His father also wrote:

Take notice my son. You have been away for more than a decade. Men go abroad to support their families, but you have not sent us money or letters since then. Everyone at home is anxious and worried, even in their dreams. I am disturbed and confused. Are you intending to let us starve to death? If you had sent no money back because of your bad business then I would not blame you. But I have been told that your business is booming, and you have made much money. Why don't you send some back? Even if you don't think of your mother and me, you should think of your wife and son. But you think only of yourself and enjoy your life alone without considering us. This is not suitable for a man of high character.

To the people of John Day, Hay *was* a man of high character. He and Leon often supported indigent Chinese in the community and even undertook the expense of sending their bones back to China for burial. Moreover, Hay frequently did not cash checks from his patients. When he was asked why, he said, "I don't need the money. They need it."

Hay also served the Chinese community's religious needs. Supplicants depended on him to intercede with Heaven on their behalf, and he helped with divinations. Inside the store was an elaborate altar on which he daily placed offerings of wine, fruit, and incense. When necessary, Hay solicited money from fellow immigrants to refurbish the altar and statues of the Gods.

During the early years of the store, he had even written to relatives in America asking for money to buy merchandise because Leon had lost all their ready cash gambling. Nevertheless, repeated entreaties from his own family remained unanswered.

Hay's attitude is hard to understand. Possibly he felt his relatives were trying to "bleed" him. Certainly a large proportion of the letters to immigrants were pleas for money from families in China who often had no conception of the realities of Gold Mountain or the difficulties and indignities suffered by Chinese immigrants. Those in China saw only their own needs and the ability of the immigrants to meet those needs and their (sometimes outrageous) demands. The willingness of the two partners to help their fellow immigrants—who fully understood and appreciated that aid—adds credence to this explanation. But why Hay did not send even a small sum home is still a mystery.

Similarly, Leon ignored letters from his father, wife, and daughter. They did not ask for money, only his safe return and the fulfillment of his duty to produce a son and heir. "You are my only son, and you are still without male offspring," his father reminded him. "Why not come before it's too late?"

His daughter added her entreaties: "I, your humble daughter, am always thinking that I have never seen my

A number of Chinese immigrants who tried retiring to China grew homesick for the free life of the frontier and returned to America. Ah Can, an herbalist and packer, never tried to go back to China. Already so old in 1920 that he had to saw his winter wood supply while sitting on a stump, he survived fourteen more years and was the last Chinese in Warrens, Idaho. (Courtesy John Carrey)

father. Last year, we—grandparents, mother and I—thought that you would come home, but we were all disappointed. Oh Father, I beg you to . . . please come back as quick as you can and let the whole family be together again."

Subsequent letters told of his father's rheumatism, his mother's blindness, and his wife's exhaustion from nursing them. Then came reports of his parents' deaths, his wife's "loneliness and desolation." One uncle wrote, "Day and night your wife is looking forward to your homecoming. She suffers illness continuously and is as thin as a toothpick." Other relatives also begged him to show compassion for his wife and daughter. Leon ignored them all.

Perhaps he had crossed the Pacific for the same reason many men and women on the East Coast headed west—to escape the strictures of traditional society. In any event, Leon reveled too much in the freedoms he enjoyed to ever consider going home. A dedicated gambler,

he played *mah-jong, fan-tan, pai-gow,* and Chinese and American card games—anything on which he could place a bet. He supported a racehorse for which he hired a professional trainer and jockey, and he took frequent trips to Portland and San Francisco, where he visited the tracks.

If Leon and Doc Hay acknowledged any family, it was the community of John Day. Men who came to the store could expect to be entertained with newspapers, magazines, novels, texts of operas, chess and checker sets, musical instruments, and a phonograph with records from Hong Kong and Berlin. Any child could count on a piece of candy or fruit. Or, if it was mealtime, an invitation to sit at the large round table, where they would be given their own bowls of rice, spoons, and forks.

The partners willingly housed and fed newcomers while helping them find work. And Leon used his English to help resolve conflicts between immigrant Chinese and United States Customs officers at ports in Oregon and Washington. He wrote letters, interpreted, and, on occasion, even provided temporary partnerships in the store for individuals seeking to circumvent the stringent Exclusion laws that barred laborers but permitted entry to merchants and their wives.

Despite the help of Leon and others like him, few Chinese could penetrate the barriers of Exclusion. And without women and children, the Chinese population of John Day declined steadily as men left to look for work elsewhere or went home to retire. The decrease in the Chinese population was not the financial blow it might have been for Leon and Hay because of their varied business interests (including bootlegging whiskey during Prohibition). When Leon died in 1940, he left almost $90,000 to Doc Hay for use during his lifetime, with the stipulation that half the estate would then go to his daughter in China.

Hay's practice and his will to live died with Leon. Virtually blind, he could not live alone, and a relative in Idaho, Bob Wah, was sent for. After Bob Wah, also an herbal doctor, moved his wife and four children into a house across the street, Hay's spirits improved, and he lived comfortably for a number of years until he fell and broke his hip.

Deeply superstitious, he refused to ride in an ambulance that had carried so many dead and dying. Friends had to borrow a station wagon for the trip to a hospital in Portland. His leg was set but it never healed properly, and he was forced to remain in a nursing home in the city, where he lingered for four years before his death from pneumonia in 1952.

By then Hay's estate had dwindled to a few thousand dollars and the Kam Wah Chung building, which he left to the city of John Day with the provision that it be made into a museum, a monument to the contributions of the Chinese to the development of eastern Oregon.

Today the building is listed on the National Register of Historic Places. Fully restored, it is open as a museum from May through October each year.

Ong Sin Sek, an herbalist and occulist in San Francisco's Chinatown, had no interest in cowboy movies. But his grandson, Theodore Tang, did. So every Saturday afternoon they went to the theatre. Fearful of germs in such a public place, Ong Sin Sek felt each chair with the palm of his hand, permitting his grandson to sit only when he located a seat that had been vacated long enough to be cool and therefore relatively germ free. (Courtesy Theodore Tang)

Wong Sing 1865–1934
From China to Fort Duchesne, Utah (Courtesy Thorne Studio)

Wong Sing,
Merchant Prince

When Wong Sing died in 1934, his mourners in Utah included high government officials and ranking army officers. Sixty Ute Indians met in solemn tribal council to extol his virtues. Friends and acquaintances gathered to share their memories of him with newspaper reporters and each other.

Maud Anderson, the daughter of a homesteader, remembered seeing Wong Sing when she was a child riding in a wagon with her family. They had just bounced over the cobblestones of the river bottom and were crossing the big red bridge that spanned the Uintah River when her father said, "Look at the Chinaman!" and stopped the team so they could take a closer look. "This was a long time ago," she said. "But I can see him now as he was then—a small slender fellow with a funny shirt we thought was fascinating. He had a small close-fitting cap and a long queue of black hair hanging to his waist. He was bending over a washtub doing laundry for the soldiers of the fort."

Neither Maud Anderson nor anyone else could remember exactly how or why Sing had first come to Fort Duchesne, Utah. Some believed he had emigrated with his father to San Francisco and was then hired as a handyman by an army officer who brought him to the post. Others claimed he went to Utah to join an old Chinese laundryman who had become too old to pick up and deliver the laundry himself. Still others said Sing had always worked alone. But all agreed he had been doing the wash for the soldiers at Fort Duchesne since 1889.

The Fort had been established three years earlier. Situated between the Native American and white settlements, it was 100 miles from the nearest railroad and could be reached only by stagecoach or freighter wagon. At that time, Utah was still a territory. The eastern half was the legal, treaty-granted home of the Utes, who included three distinct groups: the White River faction from Colorado, the Ouray, and the Uintah.

In 1884, the Federal Agent on the Uintah Reservation had called "his" Indians "the best lot of savages in America." But subsequent intratribal warfare and trouble with cowboys prompted the 400 or so white families to appeal to the Governor for protection; on

August 20, 1886, the black troops of the Ninth Cavalry arrived to establish the post and to "discipline and control the Indians" in eastern Utah, western Colorado, and southwest Wyoming.

The 275 soldiers in the six-company post were delighted to have Sing do their laundry, and he had more than enough business. Sing, a young man of twenty or so, had other aspirations. When two soldiers from the fort rented a room at the Fort Duchesne Hotel and opened a poker game, Sing eagerly accepted their invitation to join the game. "He was a dead game sport," his friend, William TenBroek, recalled. "The soldiers used to try to read his face, but he could hold four aces and never bat an eye."

Though Sing did not always win, he made enough to order a supply of inexpensive chinaware, which he packed in a little red wagon and sold to the wives of army officers and homesteaders when he delivered their laundry. With the profit, he opened a restaurant that catered to the military trade. A little later, he added a small store and set out to secure the Utes' trade.

Relations between Chinese and Native Americans in the West varied. In the Pacific Northwest, Chinese were at first welcomed as brothers, and some Chinese married Native American women. But as the numbers of Chinese increased, Native Americans came to regard them as poachers on their lands and fishing grounds, and there were often attacks and murders of Chinese by bands of Native Americans. Some whites added to the growing antagonisms by playing Chinese and Native American laborers against each other or disguising themselves as Native Americans when they raided Chinese camps. In Arizona, however, relations were generally more cordial. Quechan (Yuman) Indians sold fish to Chinese working in railroad construction camps and supplied the fuel for Chinese laundries.

Having been frequently betrayed, the Utes were deeply suspicious of Sing, but he won them over by a policy of strict honesty and fair dealing. He also became proficient in several Indian dialects. Before long, local Utes patronized the "Chinaman's store," arousing the jealousy of several white merchants, who had Sing expelled from the reservation. In support of Sing, the

Wong Bow (top) was only twelve when he arrived in Siskiyou County, California, in the 1850s. For several years he worked as a houseboy for the "boss" of a gold mine. Then he went to live with either the Yurok or Karok Indians, remaining with them for seven years before cultural differences (he couldn't adapt to the food or the fasting) drove him back to Happy Camp. His Native American wife and two sons did not go with him.

Thereafter known as "Yin Chin" (Indian) Bow, he worked as a rodeo rider and packer and also broke horses and trails. In his forties he remarried. His wife, Lai-shee (above), hated living in what she called "the wilderness." Nevertheless, she was able to defend herself and their thirteen children when necessary. During one of Bow's frequent absences, she successfully shot a marauding bear. (Courtesy Cherylene Lee)

Utes refused to have anything further to do with the white merchants, and shortly afterwards, their establishments were destroyed in a mysterious fire.

Sing built a new store on a small piece of land outside the reservation, across the river, one and one-half miles northeast of Fort Duchesne. Those who held licenses to trade on the reservation predicted failure for the "Chinaman's store." Instead, as Sing's reputation for integrity and fair prices grew, his trade extended to stockmen, businessmen, and farmers from every section of the Uintah Basin, and he shipped supplies and equipment to customers far beyond eastern Utah and the reservation.

The store became a market for furniture, general merchandise, and meat, and an agency for machinery sales. Each time Sing ran out of space, he added another building to the original without any regard to style. Nevertheless, former customers remember the store as a pleasant place to shop. Children never left without an all-day sucker personally handed to them by Sing, who often tucked a big sack of candy, apples, oranges, or nuts in with the groceries. And each year he designed, printed, and distributed calendars with a Native American motif.

By the mid-1920s, the store carried about $70,000 worth of stock. One day, a traveling salesman noticed Sing was still using an abacus—a counting frame common to Chinese merchants—to keep his accounts, and he tried to convince him to switch to an adding machine. When Sing failed to see any advantage to the machine, the salesman proposed a contest between the two, with each man totaling up a column of figures. Sing finished first, but his answer differed from that of the machine. On rechecking, the salesman discovered he had pressed a wrong key and Sing was correct!

The store had eight clerks. They remember Sing as a patient man who corrected them simply by saying, "Let's do it this way." "I was kinda backward," one clerk confessed, "and [Sing] brought that out of me. He taught me to figure, and he taught me to write better, and how to treat people and how to meet 'em. He really made something out of me."

To ride out the Depression of the 1930s, Sing had to cut back on staff and stock. But when a hard-pressed rancher asked for time in which to pay for a purchase, Sing would say, "It's not my policy to extend credit, but you need the goods, so take them." No matter how much people owed him, he never let them leave the store empty-handed. And stock that sat on the shelves a while inevitably ended up going to poor families for free.

Women going out into the street often risked kidnapping and sale into prostitution. In one case, the kidnap victim was found in a crate being shipped by rail from San Francisco to Reno. More often, however, women who were kidnapped disappeared forever. In 1866, the wife of Chen Chong, a Seattle merchant, was kidnapped by highbinders three months after their marriage. Chen Chong spent years searching for her in vain. Eventually, he gave up and moved to Honolulu, Hawaii. This photograph was taken on their wedding day. (Courtesy Washington State Historical Society)

After Sing's death, his son carried on the family business, and he was said to have "walked in his father's shoes." One customer, Doris Karren Burton, recalled, "During the Second World War, many things were hard to buy but Wing would just say, 'I don't have it, but I have it next time.' Once my father, a rancher, needed a 30-30 rifle. You could not get guns then, but we got one the 'next time.'" (Courtesy Thorne Studios)

Whenever there was a fire in the neighborhood, Sing would be there to help. He also contributed to Uintah County Hospital and did welfare work among the Native Americans. He assisted them in business transactions, and he learned their history and culture, becoming so accepted that he was allowed to photograph and film tribal customs. He then lent these pictures to Indian Service officials in an effort to increase their understanding of the tribes they served.

From all accounts, Sing knew everyone on and off the reservation, and many people proudly called themselves his friend. Yet no one seemed to know anything of his personal life. When Sing introduced a young Chinese man who arrived in Fort Duchesne in 1924 as his son, Wing, the residents were shocked. There were those who claimed Sing had never left the Uintah Basin and Wing was really a nephew. Others said he had gone back to China, married, and fathered a son and daughter before returning to Utah alone.

As a merchant, Sing would have been entitled under the Exclusion laws to have his wife and children join him. The process, however, would have been humiliating and speculative, since all incoming Chinese immigrants were detained (for weeks and sometimes years) at immigration stations, where they were forced to verify identities through interrogations and physical examinations. In one case a ~~woman~~ was denied entrance because the contour of her ear was supposedly different from that described on her affidavit. In another, public health doctors concluded that the applicant's age was twenty, not sixteen as claimed, and the young woman was therefore "fraudulent beyond question."

Mothers and children could also become separated, as in the case of the Wing family in Mercur, Utah. Dr. Sam Wing's wife, Molly, was admitted, but their children were not. For a few years, Molly remained with her husband, but she pined so much for her children in China that Dr. Wing finally insisted she return to them.

Nor could Sing have guaranteed the safety of his family in America. When drunken miners tried to abduct the daughter of a Chinese merchant in Fiddletown, California, and the merchant shot one of them, it was not the miners who were imprisoned, but the merchant. Since Chinese were not permitted to testify in court, the merchant had to depend on the corroboration of white residents to support his testimony of self-defense.

Not surprisingly, Sing never sent for his wife or daughter, only his son. Just as Sing feared, immigration officials in San Francisco refused to admit him.

Fortunately, a friend, William H. Siddoway, telegraphed Senator Reed Smoot, who convinced the officials that "things were as represented," and Wing was released.

For the next ten years father and son worked side by side. Then, on the morning of March 19, 1934, Sing was on his way to see a doctor in Salt Lake City about his rheumatism and to pick up merchandise when the truck in which he was riding overturned. Tracks on the highway indicated the truck went out of control, struck a shoulder, and rolled over six or seven times, hurling out Sing and the driver. The driver survived with a fractured skull, but Sing was killed instantly.

The *Vernal Express,* reporting on the accident, described Sing as "the merchant prince of the Uintah Basin." And his friend William TenBroek promised, "He will never die in the memory of his acquaintances and the residents of Uintah Basin."

Kong Tai Heong (left) 1875–1951
Li Khai Fai (right) 1875–1954
From Hong Kong and Canton, China, to Honolulu, Hawaii
(Courtesy Bishop Museum)

Li Khai Fai and Kong Tai Heong,
Physicians and Community Leaders

Li Khai Fai carefully re-examined his patient, a young Chinese bookkeeper. There was no denying the high fever, delirium, black spots, bleeding through the mouth, swelling in the armpits and groin. As an intern in Hong Kong during the black plague in 1894, he had seen too many victims to mistake the symptoms; he knew the consequences would be severe.

Conditions in Honolulu, Hawaii, in 1899—especially in the "native quarter," where Chinatown was located—were ripe for the quick spread of any disease. There was no sewer system and the cesspools, hidden under floors and in inaccessible places, had no vents and were never emptied. Refuse from people, dogs, chickens, and horses, the wastewater from laundries and kitchens, and the sour washings from handmade poi drained into the stagnant pools. Many of the narrow passages between buildings were roofed over, holding in the foul gases. Flies swarmed everywhere, and enormous roaches roamed over food, tables, and dishes.

The same ignorance that had created these conditions had generated deep prejudices against Western medicine. So intense was this mistrust that Chinese rarely brought a patient to a hospital until it was too late for a physician to do anything. As a result, practically all patients admitted to the Chinese Hospital went out in coffins.

As Western-trained doctors, Khai Fai and his wife, Kong Tai Heong, were targets of suspicion among their own people. In the three years since the couple had started their practice in Honolulu's Chinatown, however, Khai Fai had begun to dispel the fears of his compatriots, while Tai Heong, delivering babies, was winning over new mothers of all races with her skill, practical simplicity, and straightforward advice.

Nevertheless, their practice was still largely with poor Hawaiians and Portuguese, and the two doctors realized that their diagnosis of bubonic plague would probably destroy the seeds of trust they had worked so hard to sow among the Chinese. There was no cure for the plague, and the only known way to stop it from spreading was through sanitary fires—fires that would destroy the homes and businesses people had worked hard to build.

But as Tai Heong explained to her children years later, "A person must not fear to stand forth and speak out. A man must not cringe when he has knowledge of truth and experience. And though others may hide in shame, or in shame use stones to force him into their way, still, a man must be courageous and stand forth to protect the unknowing."

So Khai Fai immediately went to the Board of Health and reported the case. The doctors there were already aware of several cases of severe fever followed by sudden death. Yet they were skeptical of Khai Fai's diagnosis, questioning his background and qualifications, even the qualifications of his German professors at the Canton Medical College, where he and his wife had received their training.

It was not the first time their credentials had been challenged. When Khai Fai and Tai Heong had emigrated to Honolulu from China in 1896, they had not been permitted to practice medicine. For months Khai Fai had worked as a laborer in tobacco warehouses. Then Tai Heong, with the help of the Reverend Frank Damon (a former missionary to China), had persuaded the President of the Hawaiian Republic, Sanford B. Dole, to give Khai Fai and herself a chance to prove themselves as physicians.

The Board of Medical Examiners had grilled the couple thoroughly during an all-day comprehensive oral examination in which the Chinese Consul had acted as interpreter. Completely satisfied with their answers, the Board had recommended to the Minister of the Interior that licenses to practice medicine and surgery be issued, and Khai Fai and Tai Heong had been practicing since. Now Khai Fai's competence was being questioned once more.

When the Chinese bookkeeper died, Khai Fai performed an autopsy. Quietly he pointed out the conditions indicative of the plague to the members of the Board, convincing them of the accuracy of his diagnosis. Yet they still did not feel justified in making public the alarming facts. Only after five more similar deaths did the newspapers, on December 13, 1899, finally break the story that bubonic plague had invaded the city.

Of the estimated 46,000 Chinese in Hawaii before 1898, probably two-thirds were laborers on sugar or rice plantations. The "kow kow man" kept these field workers supplied with hot tea while they worked. Unwittingly, the tea drinking protected them from diseases transmitted by polluted water. Chinese food, with more vegetables, was also healthier than the meat and starch diet of Hawaiians, Europeans, and Americans. (Courtesy Bishop Museum)

When it became clear that Chinese would only bring patients to the Chinese Hospital to die, the United Chinese Society closed it and, in 1920, established the Palolo Chinese Home for indigent elderly men. The home, administered since 1926 by the Honolulu Social Service Bureau, now cares for women as well as men. (Courtesy Bishop Museum)

Doctors at that time realized that rats spread the plague, but it was not understood that the medium carrying the germ was the flea, which inoculated humans through its bite. Therefore, all persons, clothing, or objects coming in touch with a plague case were looked upon as possible means of contagion. The Board of Health placed the section of Honolulu containing Chinatown, where the first cases had been diagnosed, under strict quarantine and ordered the militia out for guard duty.

Many Chinese and Japanese house servants who had been visiting Chinatown overnight found themselves abruptly confined and with no means of support. Restaurants in Honolulu were left shorthanded. Orders for merchandise piled up. Business in Chinatown ground to a halt. Schools throughout the city were closed. The United States Army brought in all men on shore leave. Inter-island steamers in port were forbidden to leave and were placed under quarantine.

In addition to these measures, the Board of Health ordered the sanitary fires that Khai Fai had anticipated. Orders for twice-a-day inspections were also issued and vigorously enforced. Each time a case of plague was discovered, all other residents of the building were herded into the streets. Their clothing was removed and burned, and they were given antiseptic baths and new outfits, then forced to enter detention camps for a period of quarantine. The men walked; the women were taken in wagons. Their bags, boxes, and bundles of goods and chattels were taken from them to be disinfected and stored.

While Khai Fai and Tai Heong understood the need for sanitary fires, they felt the guards and inspectors were sometimes rude and intemperate. Many Chinatown residents considered the destruction of merchandise and personal belongings indiscriminate, and the United Chinese Society and the Chinese Consul lodged numerous protests with the government on their behalf. But the only response of the Minister of Foreign Affairs was that the Board of Health had "summary powers in cases of this kind."

Even those merchants who were not burned out sustained heavy losses because of disrupted business, and unemployment increased. Resentment among those quarantined mounted. On January 20, when a sanitary fire raged out of control, rumors flew that the Board of Health was purposely trying to destroy Chinatown.

Actually the fire had been properly set to eat its way against a light breeze. For one hour everything went as planned. Then the wind rose and shifted to the east, carrying blazing embers to the dry roofs of nearby

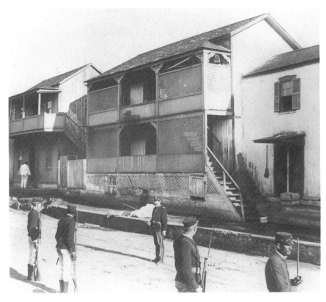

In an effort to curb the spread of bubonic plague, Honolulu's Board of Health quarantined Chinatown. A bayonet guard cordoned the district and no resident was allowed to leave without first getting a permit. (Courtesy Hawaii State Archives)

As each new case was discovered, the Board of Health sent the victim (if alive) to the Pest House. All those who had lived in the infected building were stripped and given antiseptic baths and new clothes before entering detention camp. (Courtesy Hawaii State Archives)

Furniture and household goods were removed for fumigation and the infected building was burned. (Courtesy Hawaii State Archives)

On January 20, 1900, a sanitary fire ordered by the Board of Health raged out of control, burning thirty-eight acres, almost all of Chinatown. (Courtesy Hawaii State Archives)

buildings. A shack at the back of Kaumakapili Church caught fire and sparks flew, lodging in the eastern spire. Firemen, unable to force water up to that height, tried to carry up the hose on the inside. But by then the fire had too great a hold, and they had to back down.

Flames leaped to the other spire. First one tower tottered and tumbled, then the other. The bells, tolling their own dirge as they crashed to the ground, flung sparks and embers in all directions. Wind-fanned flames vaulted fifty and sixty feet, and the conflagration swept out of control. Dense clouds of smoke rose. The heat intensified, destroying the department's best engine and forcing the firemen beyond effective fighting range. Volunteers formed bucket brigades to drench the firemen. As the water pressure decreased, dynamite charges were set off.

Hundreds and then thousands of Chinese, Japanese, and Hawaiians surged through the doomed district trying to save what they could. Most carried boxes, bags, and hastily tied bundles of valuables. In the panic, families became separated. Children cried. Women with bound feet tried to hurry and fell. Men staggered beneath the load of aged parents, sick friends. Fleeing, they found all exits blocked by guards with fixed bayonets.

Huddled on the perimeter of the infected district, not knowing where to go, what to do, or what was coming next, the refugees became increasingly frightened, angry, and resentful. The Chinese Consul and Vice Consul, special Japanese committees, and leading citizens circulated through the crush of people, soothing, explaining, calming. Fearing a riot, volunteers from outside the quarantine area rushed to help police march the 6,400 homeless to temporary shelter at Kawaiahao Church and grounds a half mile away. The escorts carried firearms, pick handles, and baseball bats—anything that might serve as a weapon. Though none of the refugees were hit, many complained of rough handling.

As soon as people outside the area learned of the thousands of homeless, gifts of food, tents, utensils, blankets, and mattresses—and use of vehicles to convey the goods—poured in. Nearly all the builders and carpenters in the city worked round the clock erecting kitchens, baths, and dormitories.

To prevent plague germs from being carried out by searchers and looters, Chinatown's smoldering ruins were enclosed with a high wooden fence. Within a month, the refugees took their final disinfecting baths and left quarantine. But the Board of Health did not declare Honolulu free of plague for another three and a half months. Although rebuilding was then permitted, those who suffered losses had to wait two years for compensation. Even then, only $850,000, half the total claimed, was awarded.

Meanwhile, the Chinese Relief Society collected funds for the care of Chinese who were unable to make a new start because they had lost everything. The Society also supplied rice twice a week to 1,000 men, women, and children until the recipients again became self-supporting.

Many Chinese blamed their heavy losses on Khai Fai for reporting the case that began the chain of unhappy events. He was forced to resign from the staff of the Chinese Hospital, and the medical practice he and Tai Heong had labored to build among the Chinese shriveled. Khai Fai blamed these reactions on ignorance and prejudice, both of which could be eradicated, he believed, through political reform in China and education in Hawaii.

His father, a preacher, had been a man of faith. Once, when confronted by a tiger, he had simply dropped to his knees to pray, and the tiger, after watching a short while, had dashed into the darkness. While Khai Fai was also a man of faith, he believed in action more than prayer. After his father had been stoned to death for being a Christian, his mother left her four children—including Khai Fai—with relatives, entered medical school, and matriculated as a doctor. She had changed her circumstances by coupling hard work with faith. So would he.

Leaving the medical practice and the burden of raising and supporting their growing family largely to Tai Heong, he became active in the Chinese Reform Movement in Hawaii. As a medical student in China, Khai Fai had been inspired by reformer Kang Yu Wei, who believed in a constitutional form of government with the emperor maintained on his throne. Now he joined Bow Wong Wui, the Protect Emperor Association. A more popular reform association was Tung Mung Wui, which supported the Hawaii-educated Dr. Sun Yat-sen, a proponent of change through revolution. But Khai Fai's loyalty to Bow Wong Wui was steadfast, and he served as editor of the association's newspaper, the *New China,* and as president for many years.

In 1911 he and other members of the association and a few young intellectuals founded the People's Ethical Training School, Mun Lun, which became the largest and best-equipped Chinese school in Hawaii, influencing generations of students. He also sought to educate

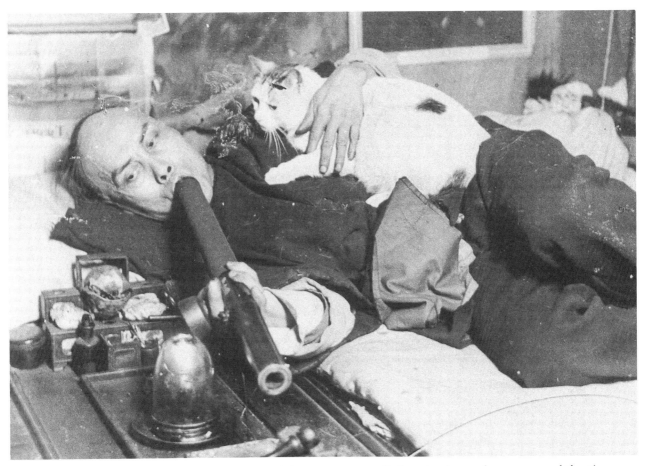

Planters only contracted for male laborers, and many of the Chinese began taking opium to escape the loneliness and monotony of life on the plantations. As one man who sought help with opium addiction explained to a social worker, "There was very little to do when work was over, and the other fellows who were having a good time smoking asked me to join them, so I took up opium smoking, not realizing that I would probably have to die with it." (Courtesy Lily Song)

Two sons and a daughter of Tai Heong and Khai Fai became medical doctors, and several of their grandchildren and great-grandchildren practice medicine today. Here Tai Heong and Khai Fai confer with their daughter, Dr. Elizabeth Li. Trained as an obstetrician and gynecologist, "Doctor Betty" worked in China during World War II. For a while she was attached to the Chinese army. Later she headed a public health station in Nanking, attending between 400 and 500 patients a day. (Courtesy Bishop Museum)

Kong Tai Heong, her name scrawled on a piece of paper pinned to her clothes, was a baby when she was left on the steps of the Berlin Mission Foundling House in Hong Kong. The top student at the orphanage, she won a scholarship to Canton Medical College, where she was considered the school's most brilliant student. Tai Heong taught her own children the Christmas carols and hymns she had learned from the nuns who raised her. For many years, she served as president of the Honolulu Chinese Orphanage Society. She also sent money back to the orphanage in Hong Kong right up to her death. (Courtesy Bishop Museum)

Tai Heong's children often accompanied her on house calls. Invariably she would also take along a gift—an embroidered handkerchief or a school bag—for the child in the household who would have to help care for the newborn infant she delivered. (Courtesy Bishop Museum)

laborers and prostitutes on the dangers of venereal disease, opening a medical office on the edge of the red-light district. And he joined other concerned leaders of the Chinese community in campaigning against the use of opium.

While the other members of the Anti-Opium League were content to hold public meetings and pay for the treatment of users, Khai Fai—believing the root of the problem lay with suppliers rather than users—reported the names of opium smugglers to the authorities. Since some of these smugglers were rich and influential, he again incurred the wrath of many in the Chinese community.

Tai Heong shared the vilification heaped on her husband, and men who opposed Khai Fai's political beliefs refused to engage her as an obstetrician for their wives. Personally, she deplored conflict of any kind. At the same time, she was never ashamed to express her opinions, and she encouraged her children to think independently and speak their ideas freely.

From 1897 to 1914 she gave birth to thirteen children, eight of whom survived. Determined to send them to private schools for the best education available and to buy a home they could call their own, Tai Heong did not stop working between babies: she could often be seen walking to the office carrying one child in her arms and another on her back. She fed them with the rice, sweet potatoes, bananas, and chickens the patients paid her in lieu of cash. She made underwear for them out of flour bags and bought cotton cloth by the bolt to make clothes for the six girls, cutting from the same pattern to save material. Somehow she still managed to find time to participate actively in church, community, and welfare work—and to teach her children how to cook and encourage them to develop their dramatic and musical talents.

Tai Heong also delivered a lot of babies. In 1946 Robert Ripley featured her in his syndicated newspaper column, "Believe It or Not," for the highest record of delivery [over 6,000] of any private practitioner."

Khai Fai shared his love of sports with their children and, according to their daughter Gladys, he "liked to quote poetry and had a great zest for living." Most important of all, perhaps, for his American-born children, "He taught us that in order to appreciate the culture of China we must learn to be good Americans first."

Many of Khai Fai's editorials in the *New China* amplified this theme, stimulating in the readers a consciousness of world problems and a concept of the Chinese community's role in Hawaii's future. "The Overseas Chinese must come to realize that they are not living in small hamlets segregated from the world about them by high walls of stone and mind," he wrote. "They must learn to think of themselves as citizens of the Territory of Hawaii, a part of the great United States of America, a country which is a part of the whole wide world! They must come to realize that what happens to the rest of the world affects not only the country of their choice, but their very own lives."

In 1946 Li Khai Fai and Kong Tai Heong celebrated their golden wedding anniversary, fiftieth year of practice, and seventy-first birthdays with over a thousand friends and relatives. Not long afterward, they died within a few years of each other, both active to the end.

❖ Generations ❖

Arlee Hen
(Courtesy Christine Choy)

Arlee Hen
and Black Chinese

Arlee Hen's parents met on the California Plantation in Mississippi, where her father, Wong On, was a sharecropper. Her mother, Emma Clay, had been born on the plantation just after Emancipation and had never left the Mississippi Delta. But Wong On, twenty years older, had run away to America from his home in Hoiping, China, when he was just a boy. Since then he had worked his way across half the continent as a water boy and then laborer on different railroads, eventually ending up in New Orleans, where he made a living from fishing and cutting cane.

In 1875 he boarded a steamboat with thirteen friends and went up the Mississippi to pick cotton in the Delta. Unable to earn enough money to send home to their families in China, Wong On and his friends formed a partnership under the name of Shing and, pooling their earnings, rented land to grow cotton.

The sharecropping system functioned to keep tenants poor and make planters rich. Paying as little cash as possible for the crops, planters would "furnish" food and seed and "deduct" necessities their tenants obtained from the plantation commissaries, where credit was extended at thirty-six percent interest. While Emma was growing up, blacks fought against this near slavery by exercising their newly won right to vote and by moving from one plantation to another, thereby forcing planters to make concessions. In response, planters tried to encourage European and Yankee immigration. When that failed, they launched a campaign to bring in Chinese.

Chinese labor was attractive because only men would be recruited, so every person would be a worker and could be cheaply housed in barracks. Moreover, since planters did not purchase Chinese outright, they would not lose capital when a man died. And, as new immigrants, the men would not be able to vote. The planters also believed that the Chinese would be less troublesome than blacks. They hoped that the presence of an alternative source of labor would intimidate blacks into resuming their pre-Emancipation positions of servitude. Those who objected to "heathens" were pointedly told by Chinese recruiter Tye Kim Orr: "You want cotton and cane and if he [the Chinese] makes them, you will not object very much."

But Chinese workers proved more expensive and rebellious than anticipated. When the political power of blacks was destroyed by white fraud and violence in 1876, the planters gave up the experiment and returned to black labor. Most of the Chinese who left the cotton fields sought work in Arkansas, Louisiana, and Georgia. The few who remained became peddlers and storekeepers.

The Shing partnership, formed just as planters were abandoning Chinese labor, refused to accept the system of "furnish and deduct" for its crop. Instead, the partners rented a boat and went to New Orleans to sell their cotton. Between times, they peddled candy, cloth, combs, and other small items to blacks on the plantations. Their daring and enterprise made them marginally better off than other sharecroppers. Nevertheless, they recognized that farming in the Delta was too similar to farming in China: ultimately, only the planter/landlord could win. In 1880, the partnership was amicably dissolved, and the other men left the area. But Wong On, in love with Emma, stayed.

Before they could marry, he had to find a way to support them. By then Wong On was well aware that the planters controlled every aspect of life on and off the plantations. Hadn't they prevented the Shing partnership from finding local buyers for its crops? Though they called him "Captain" because he had been the leader of the group, he knew the title was an empty one, almost a mockery; if he stayed in the Delta, he had to be careful not to antagonize the planters or any of the whites. At the same time, he did not want to upset blacks by competing for a job in any of the service occupations. He also wanted to earn more than the subsistence wages they were paid.

Pondering the possibilities, Wong On arrived at the same conclusion as the fifty or so Chinese already scattered in small Mississippi towns. He would open a store. Not for whites—their population was too small to support the kind of store he could afford to open—but for blacks. True, they only had money to spend on absolute basics. But if Chinese villages could support small mercantile establishments, so could towns in the Delta. The only reason there were no stores was that whites were disdainful of the small profit margin. Nor did they want to serve blacks. And blacks, kept impoverished by the system in which they had been born, couldn't scrape together the necessary capital.

During the 1880s, Chinese fishermen in the Barataria bayous of Louisiana employed Spaniards, Italians, and Mexicans; intermarried with white, black, Creole and Indian women; and generally adapted to local ways. Living and working on large wooden platforms built on pilings over the marshes, they boiled their catch in huge cauldrons of salt water, then spread the shrimp out on the platforms, raking and turning them occasionally until they were thoroughly dried. Finally, with their feet wrapped in burlap, they removed the heads and hulls by treading rhythmically on the shrimp in a process known as "dancing the shrimp." The dried shrimp was exported to China. (Illustration from Harpers, May 20, 1882)

In 1880, Wong On opened a store in Stoneville, near the California Plantation, where he was courting Emma. A twenty-by-twenty-foot shack with the grocery in the front and living quarters in the back, "Charlie's Store" was identical to the ones started by other Chinese. There was a single large counter facing the door, and the customers—blacks who came from the plantations or held menial jobs in town—asked for specific items from the stock of meat, meal, molasses, tobacco, and canned goods stacked on shelves behind the counter.

In stores where the owner could not speak English, customers used a pointer stick to indicate what they wanted. The owner saved the last package or can of each item to show the salesman from the wholesaler what he wanted to reorder. Wong On had learned to speak, read, and write a little English from a white family in Seattle shortly after his arrival from China. Though he never did speak the language fluently, he knew enough to deal with his customers—and to win Emma Clay.

Within a year of their marriage in 1881, Emma gave birth to a son. Twelve more children, nine of whom "lived to get grown," followed in quick succession. Wong On rented a house in Greenville, a town on the Mississippi River where a small number of Chinese had settled. Since the store stayed open from dawn until late at night, he continued to live in the room at the back, with Emma and the children coming out to see him whenever they could.

According to Arlee, their daughter born in 1893, she and her siblings—caught between white and black— were often lonely. Since Emma was an orphan, there were no cousins. The white children played with them when they felt like it, but only on their own terms. The black children did not like them because their parents did not fully approve of Chinese-black marriages.

At that time about thirty percent of the Chinese in Mississippi were married to black women, but the 1900 census shows only 226 Chinese in the entire state. They spread out to avoid competing with each other; most small towns, like Stoneville, could only support one store, hence one Chinese, Wong On. Though there were more Chinese in Greenville, there was only one Chinese woman and no Chinese children. Neither were there any other black Chinese children that Arlee could remember. But she did have two friends, the daughters of black women and white fathers.

All children of mixed heritage had to go to the school for blacks. "It was just miserable," she recalled. "There were no desks, just long wooden benches and one heater sitting in the middle of the floor. The teacher would let one crowd get warm, and then they would go back to their seats and the other children

Just as Chinese in the South married blacks, intermarriages occurred with Native Americans in the Pacific Northwest, Mexicans in the Southwest, and Hawaiians in Hawaii. On the West Coast, where anti-Chinese feelings were the most intense, marriages between Chinese and whites—such as this San Francisco couple—were rare. But on the East Coast, such marriages were not uncommon; the only reaction to the weddings of two Chinese men to white women in Augusta, Georgia, in 1882 was the local paper's usual good wishes for newlyweds. (Courtesy Wong Chin Foo Collection)

Generally, children of mixed marriages adopted the culture of their mothers. Some fathers, however, insisted on their children learning Chinese language and traditions. In one instance, a Chinese man took his daughter away from his Mexican wife and placed her with a Chinese family. Then, when that family proved too acculturated, he removed the child again, placing her with a family that observed Chinese customs strictly. Pictured above is a Mexican Chinese family in Benson, Arizona. (Courtesy Beuhman Memorial Collection, Arizona Historical Society)

would go and get warm; and the wind would be whistling all through the windows."

Occasionally, when Arlee passed the pretty little school for whites, "The children would come out and talk to me and bring their books out. Their books were entirely different from the books I studied. Even in the same grade we did not have the same books."

Nevertheless, she acknowledged, "I didn't feel the pinch of being colored." When she went to get fitted by her mother's sewing woman (who was white), Arlee was allowed to go through the front door, while black children had to go around to the back. Sometimes the woman's children would let Arlee read their books. And the daughter of their white neighbors often took her to the white Sunday school.

Arlee realized quite young that acceptance depended largely on coloring and features—in her case, light skin and straight "Chinese" hair. Many black Chinese, away from their hometowns where they were "known" to be black, found themselves considered Chinese or, if dark, Polynesian. Some "passed" as whites or merged into black communities. A few took advantage of the "Mexican/Indian" categories to be considered white in some situations and black in others.

From her brothers' experiences, Arlee also observed that females generally found acceptance more easily than males. "Two of my brothers looked very much like Chinese and then some of them looked more like colored, but you could see the strain of Chinese with their eyes," she recalled. "The eyes were slant, nose kind of small, no bridge." But all of them, regardless of their appearance, were "prejudiced against by three races." So as soon as they were grown, they left for St. Louis and Chicago. Arlee and her sister, however, were both accepted by the local Chinese community and never left Greenville.

Arlee had always considered herself Chinese. Her father's favorite, she had often stayed with him in the Stoneville store after the rest of the family returned to Greenville. He had raised her as a Chinese daughter, teaching her how to cook Chinese food and grow Chinese vegetables. Setting aside a section especially for Arlee in the large garden he raised each year behind the store, he gave her seeds from every variety he planted. Then, while they hoed and weeded, he told her stories about China.

Because he was only thirteen when he left, he did not remember very much. But he explained that if he cut his queue, he could never go home again. He described how, on the morning he had run away, he had gone across the lake to graze the water buffalo just as he did every day. Then he retrieved the bundle of clothes he had hidden under a bush the night before and sneaked off.

Though he had never said good-bye to his family and had even stolen money from his grandmother before leaving, Wong On stayed in touch with them, frequently writing to his sister. When Arlee was eight, her father decided to send her to China with a cousin of his who was going home. She was thrilled, but her mother screamed and cried and refused to let her go.

Her father then tried to teach her Chinese, but Arlee never picked it up. She and her sister, Eldee, were good students, however. Their mother had high aspirations for all her children and had hired the principal of the black school to give them an extra two hours of tutoring every afternoon. But when the planters learned that the principal taught racial equality, they forced him to leave town. The strong foundation he had already laid enabled Eldee to complete twelfth grade and become a teacher, a rare accomplishment in those days.

Arlee's education was cut short after she came down with typhoid fever at the age of twelve. In a coma for almost three months, she was unable to walk for another two years. For a while after she recovered, she helped out at the Stoneville store. Then she went to work at the largest grocery in Greenville, Joe Gow Nue No. 1.

Little had changed in the thirty years since her father had come to the Delta. As Arlee later recalled, "The country people worked on shares, and every month they received an allotment. A family would buy a twenty-four-pound sack of flour, a twenty-four-pound sack of meal, perhaps an eight-pound bucket of lard, and the rest above the small things that they didn't raise in the country, but it was such a meager allowance that they couldn't buy anything that would be considered a luxury—nothing, not even the things they really needed, they couldn't have."

Nevertheless, on Saturdays customers crowded into groceries all over Mississippi, and there was enough profit to encourage more Chinese to come. Generally, new arrivals were relatives who worked at their cousins' and uncles' stores until they learned the rudiments of the operation and enough English to set up their own businesses with a combination of savings, loans, and credit from the wholesalers they met during their training. Beginning on a firmer financial footing than the Chinese of Wong On's generation, many of the new arrivals were able to save enough to send to China for

The feelings of loneliness expressed by Arlee Hen were not unique to black Chinese. Edith Eaton, the daughter of a Chinese mother and English father, felt tormented by the way in which she and her thirteen siblings were treated, whether in England, America, or Canada. In her autobiographical Leaves from the Mental Portfolio of an Eurasian, *she wrote, "Older persons pause and gaze upon us, very much in the same way that I have seen people gaze upon strange animals in a menagerie." In school, children refused to sit beside Edith and her siblings. Before and after school, she later recalled, "There were pitched battles, of course, and we seldom leave the house without being armed for conflict." Yet she never shared these problems with her parents because "they would never understand. How could they? He is English, she is Chinese. I am different to both of them—a stranger, though their own child." (Courtesy* International Examiner)

Inevitably, culture clashes sometimes led to separations and divorce, as in the case of Wong Aloiau and his half-Hawaiian, half-German wife, Emma Kalikokauai Ellis, seen here with their daughter Rose. (Courtesy Daphne Kong Apana and Violet L. Lai)

wives rather than marrying local women. When the children of these marriages grew to school age, the Chinese began to demand changes.

Unwilling to have his American-born daughters forced to attend the inferior black schools, Lum Gong—a grocer in Rosedale—went to court in 1924. His lawyers argued successfully in the Circuit Court that Lum Gong's daughter, Martha, "is not a member of the colored race nor is she of mixed blood. She is pure Chinese." The Mississippi Supreme Court—stating that the white race is limited to Caucasians and that all other races, including Chinese, were "colored"—overturned the decision. The United States Supreme Court affirmed the appellate ruling, claiming that the distinction was necessary "to preserve the purity and integrity of the white race and prevent amalgamation and to preserve as far as possible the social system of racial segregation."

To the Chinese in Mississippi, the message of these court decisions was clear: If they wanted an education and a future for their children, they would have to ally themselves with the white race and dissociate from the black.

Emulating whites, the Chinese created separate schools for their children. They established youth organizations that paralleled those of the white community. They became Christians. Since most of the whites were Baptists, that was the denomination the majority of Chinese selected. Baptist missionaries aided in this effort and, according to one convert, "The Baptist religion is very much like the Chinese religious way of thinking. You know, no smoking, drinking, and gambling. Also, the Baptists believe in keeping the family close together, like Chinese families do. So we converted over to the Baptist way of thinking pretty easy. It was very much like the Chinese way we were taught at home."

Separating themselves from the blacks was more difficult. They were dependent on blacks for their income and could not relocate their stores. But whenever possible, they moved out of their living quarters at the back of the groceries. Though some families were refused houses in areas of their choice, most were able to buy in working-class neighborhoods. As one Chinese put it, "The money's not Chinese. It still has George Washington's picture on it."

"Pure" Chinese then cut themselves off from those who had married blacks. "We didn't try to break up their marriages," they told interviewers. "We didn't have anything to do with them, that's all. We just didn't invite them to our houses or parties." The rights they fought for were only for "pure" Chinese. When the Greenville public school for whites finally admitted

Rose and her sister Mollie (on either side of Wong Aloiau)
remained with their father and were raised by his next
wife, Mew Hin Tam. (Courtesy Daphne Kong Apana and
Violet L. Lai)

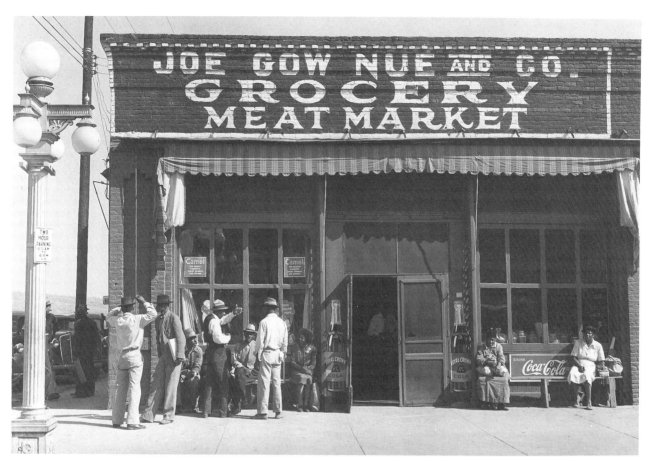

A *few of the Chinese groceries, like the Joe Gow Nue Store, where Arlee Hen worked, became so successful that the owners opened additional stores in other towns, starting small chains. Today, most of the old groceries have given way to modern superettes and liquor and drug stores. Many Delta Chinese are professionals—doctors, lawyers, and architects—who* serve *as church deacons and on the boards of banks and business associations. A few even hold public office. But the Chinese number 2,000—less than one percent of the population— and their "place" in the social structure is still somewhere between black and white. (Courtesy Library of Congress)*

Chinese children in 1940, students had to prove that they did not have "one drop of black blood."

Blacks also exerted pressure against Chinese-black marriages. According to one Chinese married to a black, "[The blacks] know my wife, they grew up with her, but because of the name, they ostracize her. We can't even hire a babysitter." Chinese-black marriages therefore became increasingly rare, and most black Chinese moved away.

Arlee and her sister both married Chinese. While Arlee spoke of black disapproval, she could not recall any problems from the Chinese community over her marriage to Joe Suen Heung in 1929. She and her husband changed their surname to Hen and, with the help of Wong On, opened a store, J. S. Hen & Co. Like other Chinese groceries of the period, it was a place for friends to meet, drink a beer, or leave children while doing errands. Though customers often passed large portions of their day there, the sums of money they spent were small, so the owners' hours were long. Opening by four in the morning to catch business from the field workers, they did not close until ten or eleven at night.

On Sundays all the stores closed, and Chinese grocers would come and visit the Hens just as they used to visit Wong On. When the men died (Wong On in 1943 and Joe Suen Hen in 1975), "The Chinese people were right there. They took over the burial arrangements just like they were members of the family."

After her husband's death, however, the visits to Arlee stopped, though two Chinese women did continue to bring her food. There were visits from the black women of her church and from her sister's son, James, and his wife, who cooked Chinese food for Arlee. But there were no friends.

When interviewed by Chinese, she insisted, "I never did feel any difference from Chinese." But she told a black interviewer, "As a rule, you know, Chinese people, whether they know each other or not—it is just like a brotherhood. It's not like other people, especially our people."

During the first half of Arlee's long life, her first statement may well have been true. When she died in 1985, her latter statement proved the more accurate, for she was refused burial beside her husband because the Chinese cemetery is for "pure-blooded" Chinese only.

During the two years their case was being tried in the courts, Berda and Martha Lum did not attend school. Afterward, rather than try to raise the money for a segregated Chinese school, their father moved the family to Arkansas, where the girls resumed their disrupted education.
In 1936, Delta Chinese—with the support of several churches—raised $25,000 to build the Chinese Mission School, which included dormitories to accommodate out-of-town students. Though not equal to the white schools, it was superior to the schools for blacks and the one-room Chinese schools which operated only sporadically. Like other Chinese schools in the Delta, this one in Indianola was taught by a white teacher, Mary Tom Pearson. These teachers were often subjected to harsh criticism from their communities for teaching Chinese children. (Courtesy Mississippi Department of Archives and History)

Chin Lung, his wife Leung Kum Kew, and six of their nine children
(Courtesy Tom Bick Fong)

Chin Lung's
Gold Mountain Promise

Some time in the early 1880s, Chin Hong Dai—known as Ah Lung, or Dragon—left his village of Namshan for America, the land known as Gold Mountain. Close to twenty years old, he was too weak from hunger to hold up a bucket of urine to fertilize the fields without his sister's help. There wasn't enough money to buy sufficient fabric to make a proper pair of trousers, so he wore the short pants of a boy. Yet he was confident that if he just worked hard enough, he would succeed. As he told a grand-nephew years later, "It was important to be optimistic. Otherwise there would be no hope or future."

He started out working at Sing Kee, a rice-importing store in San Francisco with branches in a number of Chinatowns in the mining regions. The rice Ah Lung threshed and bagged each day sold for six dollars a sack. Wages at that time averaged one dollar a day plus board. Clearly the people who made money were not laborers but those who owned their own businesses. Ah Lung also believed a knowledge of English would be useful in getting ahead. So, intent on making true the promise of Gold Mountain, he studied English at the Chinese Baptist Church at night.

His opportunity for self-employment came a few years later when landowners from the Sacramento–San Joaquin delta went to San Francisco to look for tenant farmers. As early as 1852, Chinese, Native American, and Hawaiian labor had been used to build levees in the delta. After turning the marshland into one of the richest agricultural regions in California, many of the Chinese laborers had begun to farm. Often Chinese from the same area worked together, and since Ah Lung could speak English, a group of men from his district asked him to go with them to the delta.

The land had to be drained and diked before they could plant, so the first years were extremely difficult. Though the food Ah Lung ate in America was better than the diet of yam gruel at home, he was still not a strong man. His hands and feet became so bloody while he was reclaiming land that he cried himself to sleep at night. Nevertheless, he kept at it. By being extremely frugal—outside of food and shelter he spent less than a dollar a month—he was able to save enough to go home and marry before he was thirty.

Farming in the delta was a relatively stable and economically satisfactory occupation that allowed the men involved to bring their wives to America—if they could find a way to circumvent the Exclusion laws. Over the years Ah Lung had invested his savings in Sing Kee, and he was probably able to pose as a merchant in order to bring his bride, Leung Kum Kew, back with him.

So few Gold Mountain wives were able to join their husbands in America that Cantonese folk songs of the period warned:

> If you have a daughter, don't marry her to a Gold
>   Mountain man.
> Out of ten years, he will not be in bed for one.
> The spider will spin webs on top of the bedposts,
> While dust fully covers one side of the bed.

But there were no warnings about the hardships wives would face in America.

While the men enjoyed strong community support through work, communal living, and the formation of clan associations, Chinese women lived in isolation. Confucian ethics confined high-born women to their homes, while child care, household chores, and wage-earning work (usually done at home) imprisoned wives whose families depended on their financial contributions. Though hardest on those with bound feet—one woman in Idaho remembers watching her mother flatten her twisted feet by smashing them with bricks—there were few pleasures for any. So endless was the drudgery these women endured that one wife and mother in Pennsylvania was able to leave the family laundry only three times in thirty-eight years.

Ah Lung's wife, Leung Kum Kew, intensely disliked life in America. The delta, a breeding ground for malaria, was not a healthy place to live. Neither did the fine peat dust that permeated everything, including skin, make for a pleasant environment. Kum Kew therefore stayed in San Francisco and Ah Lung visited whenever he could. Their first child, a daughter, was born in 1892. Three more babies followed in quick succession. Because Kum Kew had bound feet, a young *mui-tsai*, slave girl, was purchased to help with the

Ah Lung, according to his nephew Chin Wun Leung, was frugal when it came to his own needs but generous when it came to the needs of others. At his eightieth birthday celebration, even beggars were given a table at the banquet, and he donated generously to public works for the village and helped dozens of relatives. After a bad harvest, Ah Lung waived his nephew's rent. "Don't be discouraged," he told Chin. "I was only successful because others helped me." (Courtesy Tom Bick Fong)

babies and household chores. To help make ends meet, Kum Kew took in sewing.

Finally, in 1898, Ah Lung was able to sign his first lease—for 200 acres on a sharecropping basis—in his own name. Two years later he leased 1,125 acres for $7,000. Within a few years he was leasing tracts of land all over the delta, primarily to grow potatoes but also beans, onions, asparagus, and hay (for his seventy farm horses).

Ah Lung, known as the Potato King, attributed his success to his own self-confidence and others' confidence in him. "It was a matter of honesty, diligence, and opportunity," he said. Well liked and respected by whites, he acknowledged the help of three in particular: an Italian banker, Scatena, whom he called his "long-time friend"; an Irishman, Green, who helped by "explaining things"; and a grain merchant, John M. Perry, who lent him the money he needed for operating expenses when he was getting established.

Ah Lung's own abilities should not be underestimated, however. Though virtually illiterate, he had an excellent memory. His knowledge of English enabled him to communicate with landlords and creditors and to sell his crops. His abilities as a negotiator brought him the best prices. And he was open to new ideas and technology, purchasing a tractor and a potato-washing machine.

Knowing how hard life was at home, Ah Lung gave preference to hiring relatives and men from his own district, often paying their passage. "If he sponsored you to work for him for over three years, he would give you $600 a year to send home and cover your meals," a villager from Nam San explained. "So people wanted to come and work for him. After three years of working for him, you were on your own."

Since potato cultivation does not require specialized labor, only the cooks, foremen, teamsters, and grooms for the horses were hired year-round. Five hundred laborers worked seasonally. "In Stockton, if you simply said so many people were needed at a certain camp, someone would transport them there in horse carts," Ah Lung's son recalled. The same was true in other delta Chinatowns. These workers were paid the going daily wage of one to two dollars a day and board, but Ah Lung paid the skilled laborers five dollars a day. He also gave some men the option of becoming partners rather than working for wages.

His flexibility and sensitivity toward the circumstances of others extended to his relationship with his wife. In 1904, he gave in to her wish to leave America, and for the next two decades he commuted across the

Pacific between his work and his family, making fourteen trips.

Instead of going back to Ah Lung's village, Kum Kew settled in the Portuguese colony of Macau, an hour's boat ride from Namshan. There were several reasons for this decision. Most importantly, families with relatives overseas were favorite targets of the bandits who plagued the Chinese countryside. Ah Lung reputedly paid them protection money. Nevertheless, it was safer to stay in Macau, which was under foreign jurisdiction.

Living in Macau was also more comfortable. Kum Kew could easily afford to purchase a spacious two-story house with indoor plumbing, something even the wealthiest homes in rural China were without. The slave girl she had brought back from America was of marriageable age, and fulfilling her obligation as a mistress, Kum Kew found the girl a husband so she could establish a home of her own. She then bought four more slave girls—slaves were available for a few dollars apiece and often were free—and hired a male gardener, a cook, and kitchen helpers.

With plenty of household help and no sewing, Kum Kew had the hours of leisure she could only dream of in America. She used that time to learn how to read and write in Chinese. After converting to Christianity, she was appointed chair of the women's group at the church. She also unbound her feet.

Meanwhile, Ah Lung struggled to keep hold of his farming empire. Like many Chinese in America, he recognized that the protection of his rights and property depended on a strong China. He therefore joined the Chinese Reform Movement, which sought to change the inept and corrupt Manchu government. According to Captain Ansel O'Banion, an Irish American active in the movement, Ah Lung even used his "potato boats"— barges that transported his produce—to smuggle Dr. Sun Yat-sen, China's George Washington, and other would-be revolutionaries into San Francisco.

In 1911, the Manchu government was overthrown. But as politicians and warlords in China wrangled for power in the new republic, the lot of the Chinese in America deteriorated. In 1913, the year after Ah Lung finally saved enough money to buy his first piece of land (1,100 acres northwest of Stockton), California passed the Alien Land Act, which prohibited "aliens ineligible for citizenship" from buying land in the state. Since Chinese were barred by law from ever becoming naturalized citizens, Ah Lung could no longer purchase land in California. He bought 2,000 acres in Klamath Falls, Oregon, farming simultaneously in Oregon and Califor-

Families with relatives overseas were special targets of the bandits and warlords that plagued Kwangtung Province. Lew Yao Huan—Virginia Military Institute, Class of 1925— had a special interest in exterminating the bandits, for his own mother had been attacked while he was away. A bound-foot woman, she had held off the bandits by shooting at them with a pair of pistols, one in each hand. Others, however, were not as courageous or lucky. There was a large rock known as tong yun sek, *butcher rock, where bandits took their kidnap victims and sliced off ears and fingers to encourage prompt ransom payments, murdering the victims if their demands were not met. Despite antiquated equipment and poorly trained soldiers, Lew Yao Huan successfully rid four counties of bandits through strategy and determination. (Courtesy Lew Yao Huan)*

Following custom, Chew Law Ying went to live with her husband's mother in Sei Pei Village after their marriage. "I never had to go out into the fields and do such hard work before. But mother-in-law forced me to work, carrying manure and urine and watering vegetables even when I became pregnant." After six months, Law Ying wrote her husband, Tom Yip Jing, who had returned to America to earn the money for her passage. "I told him I couldn't take it anymore. He knew his mother had an evil heart and he sent me money to move back to Macau." There she gave birth to their eldest daughter, Bick Heung. The child was three before Yip Jing saved and borrowed enough money to send for them. In this family photograph, Bick Heung is in the center, rear, See Heung is to her left, and Geem Wah is between Law Ying and Yip Jing. (Courtesy Tom Bick Fong)

nia. He also diversified his interests, opening a general import/export company and a luggage factory in San Francisco and a branch of Sing Kee in Sacramento. In his best year he earned $90,000, and even in an ordinary year his income averaged between $40,000 and $60,000. But the times were against him.

In 1920, California extended its Alien Land Law to restrict Asians from leasing land for agriculture; and in 1923, Oregon passed an Alien Land Law similar to California's. At that point Ah Lung began buying land in China. He also purchased stock in an electric company, a textile factory, a railroad, the Wing On department store in Shanghai, and buildings in Macau. When his leases in California expired and he could not renew them, he sold the land he owned in America, turned his businesses over to his sons, and retired to China.

While her husband was in America, Kum Kew enjoyed an independence that would otherwise have been denied. With the money Ah Lung sent home, she purchased property in Macau, acquiring over a dozen stores and several houses. She also managed their land in the village, going back once a year at harvest to administer the collection of rent from the tenants.

As a "Gold Mountain widow," her independence was justified. But she brought up her children to follow the traditional roles for men and women. As each of her five sons came of age to work, she sent him to his father in America. When her two daughters reached womanhood, she found them husbands. Neither marriage was successful: the younger daughter was widowed a month after the wedding and the older, Ah Kam, became impoverished due to a profligate brother-in-law.

Traditionally, a married daughter was no longer her parents' responsibility, but Kum Kew did not turn Ah Kam away when her daughter asked for help. Nor did she permit Ah Kam to live at home year-round. So Ah Kam drifted back and forth between her husband in the village and her mother in Macau. Similarly, Ah Kam's daughter, Chew Law Ying, although raised by Kum Kew, had to share a bedroom with the slave girls. She grew up in luxury but had to quit school after the primary grades because educating a girl who would eventually marry was considered wasteful. And, since marriages should be "like bamboo doors facing bamboo doors" (well matched in class and background), the groom Kum Kew selected for her granddaughter was a poor man because Law Ying's parents were poor, though her grandparents were rich.

Law Ying, having absorbed all the traditional values, entered the marriage willingly. "[Besides] Tom Yip Jing was a Gold Mountain man, and that's what mat-

Florence Ruth Tom (center), born in Colusa, California, in 1901, was given away twice. Her natural parents already had five children, so they gave her to a couple with only one son (far right). Her adoptive mother, Tom Yook Kim (second from right), doted on Florence, and when the girl became sick with a prolonged illness, she gave the child to another woman (second from left) in the hope of fooling the Gods who were making the girl ill. The trick was successful, and after Florence recovered, she returned to her adoptive mother.

Florence's adoptive father, Tom Gar Wuey, was an herbalist who also ran a small store. Her adoptive mother worked as a cook. The only Chinese girl in town, Florence was pampered by her adoptive parents and all the Chinese in Colusa's two-block Chinatown. She was given art and violin lessons, and when she graduated from high school she went on to the University of California at Berkeley, where she majored in public health. While at school, Florence agreed to an arranged marriage with Tang Tso Yam, a political science major, who was the son of a good friend and colleague of her adoptive father. They settled in Berkeley, and Florence continued to attend classes while raising a family.

During high school, Florence had won a car for selling the most magazine subscriptions. Actually, she had figured out that buying the necessary number of subscriptions was cheaper than the cost of a car, so she had bought all the subscriptions herself. An excellent driver, she frequently took her family, including her adoptive parents, on motor trips. (Courtesy Theodore Tang)

Leah Hing, born in Portland in 1907, grew up on a farm near Salem, Oregon. While still in high school, she and five other girls formed a band. After graduation, they toured major cities in the United States and Canada for one and a half years as part of "Honorable Wu's" vaudeville troupe. When the band broke up after the tour, Hing took flying lessons, earning a pilot's license in 1934 and buying her own plane. During World War II, she was an instrument mechanic at a Portland air base. She then worked for a local flying club until her retirement in the 1970s. (Courtesy Oregon Historical Society)

tered," she explained. "Everyone said life in America was good, except grandmother. I didn't believe her. Other people said going to America was like going to Heaven."

The "heaven" Law Ying went to in 1941 was a shack on an estate in Menlo Park, California, where Yip Jing worked as a gardener; he also spent grueling ten-hour days as a field laborer at a flower farm. Toiling under a blazing sun, cooking dinner over a wood-burning stove, or tossing on the soiled mattress left by the previous tenant, Law Ying dreamed of the success her grandparents had achieved, the success they promised would be hers if she worked hard.

"When you go to America, don't be lazy. Work hard and you will become rich," her grandmother had told her. "It's easy to change your circumstances if you stick to it," her grandfather said. So Law Ying worked at the flower farm and then in the sewing factories, and Yip Jing worked as a gardener and then as a dishwasher, cook, and janitor.

They might have succeeded if there had been fewer mouths to feed. But Law Ying had been brought up to believe that giving birth to a son was a woman's most important duty. Sons kept alive the family name, contributed to their parents' support, and performed ancestral worship. According to one of many Chinese proverbs on the subject, "Eighteen gifted daughters are not equal to one lame son." Law Ying therefore felt obligated to keep trying after each "failure."

The eldest daughter, Bick Heung, was born in a hospital in Macau where they had the best care modern medicine could provide. The second, See Heung, was born in the Menlo Park shack. "My water bag broke but the baby wouldn't come out," Law Ying recalled. "It was cold and raining. We lit the kerosene lamp and burned wood in the stove. An old Caucasian midwife was called to help. She felt my womb and left."

There was no question of trying to go to a hospital. Apart from the expense, it was March of 1942. Japanese Americans were being "relocated," and Law Ying and Yip Jing, unable to speak English, were afraid they would not be able to convince the military at the roadblocks that they were Chinese and not Japanese. So they waited for the midwife to return. In her eighties, the woman's hands shook so badly that Yip Jing had to help in the delivery and cut the umbilical cord.

Law Ying, determined to produce a son, was equally determined never again to give birth outside a hospital. At her insistence, the family moved into a two-room apartment in San Francisco's Chinatown. There was no

94

hot water or bathtub, and they had to share a community toilet and kitchen. Sewing at home because she could not leave the children, she earned a little over a dollar a day, less than the twenty-five cents an hour she had made at the flower farm. But she was able to give birth to the rest of her children—three within three years—at the Chinese Hospital.

See Heung, only five when her mother returned from the hospital with the fifth daughter, clearly remembers her mother weeping as she dyed the red eggs that would announce the birth to friends and relatives. Actually, Law Ying wanted to give the baby to a childless neighbor, but her husband, Yip Jing, refused to permit it. As it turned out, the baby "brought a son," for the next child was the long-awaited boy, Geem Wah. Yip Jing, suffering from a bleeding ulcer, was unable to work at the time, and the family was barely scraping by on savings. Nevertheless, he gave a fourteen-table banquet "to celebrate the arrival of Geem Wah the King."

Now more than ever Law Ying fought to fulfill the promise of Gold Mountain. "I used to think my mother didn't need to sleep," See Heung recalled. "When I went to bed, she was hunched over the sewing machine, and when I woke in the morning she was still there." Sometimes Law Ying would shake See Heung awake in the middle of the night to help her "turn out" the sashes and belts she had finished sewing. "It's all your fault I have to work so hard," she would scold. "If you had been a boy I could have stopped having children."

Supporting the six children was a struggle in which the two older girls, Bick Heung and See Heung, were expected to share. By the time See Heung was seven, she was working for wages. Bick Heung, who was four years older, had been given a job shelling shrimp after school and on weekends. Too shy to go by herself, she took along See Heung, who was put to work also. To be a working child in Chinatown in the late 1940s and early 1950s was the norm, and the girls later did housekeeping for white families during the school year and field labor at flower farms during their summer vacations, turning over all their earnings to their parents.

Law Ying had begun working at a sewing factory as soon as the children were old enough to look after one another, bringing home additional piecework to finish at night. Yip Jing, a janitor at the Mark Hopkins Hotel, worked either the early or graveyard shifts. On those inevitable occasions when the children had to be left alone, Law Ying or Yip Jing would lock them into the apartment from the outside. Just as inevitably, the children figured out how to get out.

One night, when both parents were away from home, Geem Wah went out to play with some friends. Jumping off a garage roof on a dare, he landed on a metal spike. The boy, then ten, was more afraid of his parents' wrath than the pain, and somehow he persuaded his friends to help pull out the spike, though it had penetrated his groin so deeply his colon and bladder were both punctured. For one night and a day he was able to hide his secret. Then he became so sick that he had to confess. By then infection had set in, and he sank into a coma for two weeks, suffering irreversible brain damage and cerebral palsy.

When he was finally able to come home for weekends, the family settled into a rigid routine that revolved around Geem Wah's needs. There was nothing new about deferring to him. Before the accident, the five daughters had shared a single pair of skates while Geem Wah enjoyed a bicycle of his own. They had eaten leftover rice while he ate newly cooked rice. They had worked while he played. And though it did not seem likely that he would ever fulfill the duties and obligations of a son, he was still King. When a visitor asked Yip Jing, "How many daughters do you have?" See Heung answered, "My father has no daughters, only one son."

The weight of Geem Wah's illness fell heaviest on See Heung. Bick Heung, married right out of high school, was tied down with two children of her own and another on the way. So See Heung, as the oldest daughter at home, had to act as interpreter between doctors, nurses, and social workers and her parents. Though she was only seventeen and just out of high school, she was expected to do more than translate. She had to help make the decisions for her brother's treatment. When he was able to come home, she also helped nurse him, fitting in her college classes and part-time job around his schedule.

Law Ying and Yip Jing poured their life savings into the best medical care their money could buy. But Geem Wah's condition continued to deteriorate. They ran out of money and it seemed as if the family might have to move into a housing project, in which case See Heung would not be able to live at home and would have to drop out of college. Years earlier, Law Ying had forced See Heung to give up Chinese school for an after-school housekeeping position. But now that See Heung was the first member of the family to go to college, she and Yip Jing wanted her to remain in school if at all possible. Finally admitting that Geem Wah would never recover, they hospitalized him. See Heung, taking on a

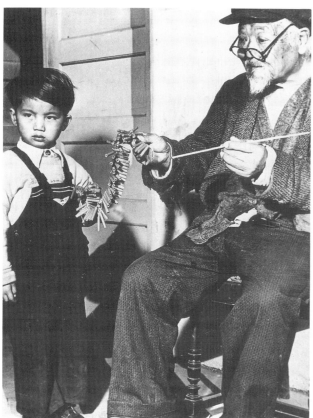

The pursuit of the Gold Mountain Promise, or American Dream, is common to most immigrants. What it means to American-born George Ow, Jr., is that "you can come from humble beginnings and become anybody and anything that you work hard and smart enough at; and when you become {this} you shall assist others." Though Ow (left) moved out of Chinatown in Santa Cruz, California, when he was eight, he well remembers the old pioneer bachelors—like Chin Lai (right)—who showered him with firecrackers, candy, stories, and love. "{The pioneers} didn't have the opportunities I've had. It was illegal for them to buy land, and there weren't good paying jobs for them. So in a sense, I feel as though I'm living out their lives doing the things they could not do."

A successful businessman, he has primary responsibility for managing family-owned shopping centers and numerous smaller developments. He also supports dance, drama, film, sculpting, and writing projects, and provides funding for annual American Dream and Women Unlimited scholarships. He is seen here (front, far right) with some winners of the American Dream scholarships. The medals worn by the recipients are inscribed "Scholarship, Achievement, Promise." (Courtesy George Ow, Jr.)

second job, successfully completed a bachelor's and then master's degree in recreation. "At my graduation," she said, "my mother was so proud that she kissed me for the first time that I can remember."

Feeling her parents' shattered hopes as intensely as if they were her own, See Heung made it her goal to give them at least a fragment of the dream with which her mother had arrived in America. With the agreement that each sister would assume mortgage payments for three years, she helped them buy a house.

Today, the house is paid for. Law Ying and Yip Jing are both retired. They live comfortably, and one of their grandchildren has already given them a great-grandchild. But none will bear the family name.

"I remember crying so much my first years in America," Law Ying said. "Life was so harsh. But today I have no regrets about leaving Macau."

"Of course you want to hit it rich," Yip Jing added. "I became rich in the sense that I could earn a living. Shelter, food, and spending money are all resolved. But not my problem in the hospital."

In 1895, Betty Woon Jung's great-grandfather, Jung Pui Lun (above), jumped ship in Monterey, California. His older brother, having failed to strike gold, had opened a laundry in Arizona, and Pui Lun joined him. Shortly afterward, his brother retired back to China. But Pui Lun, having entered the country illegally, had no papers, no possibility of going home to visit his wife (right) and son. Then, in 1906, the great earthquake and fire in San Francisco burned all the city records. Pui Lun seized the opportunity to claim American citizenship for himself and three sons, two of them fictitious, under the surname Tom. With these new papers, he went home for a brief visit. In 1913, he made a second journey home, this time for his son's marriage. (Courtesy Betty Woon Jung)

The Jung Family Album

Betty Woon Jung emigrated from Hong Kong to the United States in 1960. Technically, she is a first-generation American. In fact, she is fourth generation transplanted, for her paternal great-great-uncle emigrated from the family village of Woon Ben in Toishan not long after the Gold Rush.

For families like Betty's that have been separated for several generations, little is known about the individual members. They exchanged few letters; visits home were rare. But there were photographs, and with them, fragments of information.

Following are photographs from the Jung family album. The skeletal history they reveal is typical of the many families separated by economic and political circumstances beyond their control.

Even with papers, a villager who left for Gold Mountain could never be certain of returning home. So, to ensure the continuation of the family lineage, Pui Lun waited for his son, Sek Wah, to produce a boy child before they left for America. It took exactly one year. Then, using up all the slots he had claimed after the earthquake, Pui Lun returned to Arizona with his own son, Sek Wah, and two other male relatives. All four worked in the laundry until 1920, when Pui Lun sold the business and retired to China. Sek Wah—now the only source of the remittances on which his parents, wife, and children depended—worked as a waiter in San Francisco. After ten years, he saved enough to return home for a three-year visit during which his son, Yuk Kwun, married Tam Fung Yung, a young woman from a nearby village. (Courtesy Betty Woon Jung)

After the birth of a son and daughter, Yuk Kwun went to try his luck in Gold Mountain, landing in San Francisco in 1937. Because of the Depression, he was barely able to scratch out a living—as janitor, houseboy, and grocery clerk—until his father and two partners opened a restaurant in Monterey in 1941 and he went to work for them. Within a year, however, he was drafted into the Air Force. (Courtesy Betty Woon Jung)

Though Yuk Kwun was stationed in different parts of China, he was not able to visit his family. But after the war, he went home for eighteen months. He brought home a bicycle for his son, a boy of ten, and a wireless for the whole family to enjoy. (Courtesy Betty Woon Jung)

When his second daughter, Betty, was born, he bought her an American stroller, rocking horse, and Western clothes from the best stores in Canton. Then, in order to support his growing family, he had to return to America. (Courtesy Betty Woon Jung)

Shortly after Yuk Kwun left, another son was born, and this family photograph was sent to Pacific Grove, California, where Yuk Kwun was working in a new restaurant his father and partners had opened. His wife is holding their youngest son, Bill; his mother is holding Betty. Behind them (from left to right) are Yuk Kwun's youngest sister and brother and his older son and daughter. (Courtesy Betty Woon Jung)

In 1952, Yuk Kwun became a partner in a third restaurant opened by his father in Carmel. It should have been a happy time for him, but he was too concerned about his family in China to enjoy his success. Soon after the Communists came into power, Yuk Kwun's older daughter and son, who were in school in Canton, were taken to Hong Kong by relatives. Unfortunately, the money Yuk Kwun had sent for train fares for his mother, wife, and younger children had been used by other members of the family to buy passage for themselves. (Courtesy Betty Woon Jung)

Four generations of villagers had envied the luxuries and land the Jungs' remittances had bought. Now, under the new government, these villagers confiscated the property, imprisoned Yuk Kwun's mother, turned his wife and children out of the family home, and assigned Fung Yung to forced labor. Leaving Betty, who was three, in charge of the baby, Fung Yung set out each day to build roads. She transported load after load of dirt on her back—and planned escape. First, she petitioned the authorities for permission to move to Canton. By the time permission was granted, Betty was old enough for kindergarten, and while her daughter sang, "I am Mao's little soldier," Fung Yung looked for a woman she could trust who would be willing to take Bill to Hong Kong as her own son. Then, after he was safely out of the country, Fung Yung told the authorities her husband was visiting in Hong Kong and asked permission to take their daughter to see him. The authorities, believing young Bill was in Canton (thereby guaranteeing Fung Yung's return), granted permission. Just as Bill was not in Canton, Yuk Kwun was not in Hong Kong, but Fung Yung had succeeded in reuniting with her children. Her ingenuity could not get them to America, however. (Courtesy Betty Woon Jung)

For some reason no one in the family can recall, Yuk Kwun had emigrated as a single man. Now he could not claim a wife and four children. In 1958, he was able to secure false papers for his eldest child, who joined him in Carmel. But when his father began processing papers for his mother to join them, the lies of fifty years started to unravel. Their lawyer advised Yuk Kwun and his father to take advantage of the State Department's Confession Program and admit to their false name and papers. After confession, they were able to take back their true surname, Jung, and mother, wife, younger daughter, and son were cleared for immigration. However, Yuk Kwun's older girl, Ngon Woon, was denied entry. Finally, in 1961, their lawyer was able to persuade a senator to pass a private law "For the relief of Jung Ngon Woon." The following year, Ngon Woon arrived in San Francisco, where this photograph was taken. For the first time in almost a century, the Jung family was reunited not just for a visit, but for life. (Courtesy Betty Woon Jung)

Lai Yun Oi
(Courtesy Him Mark Lai)

The Lai Family,
Reclaiming History

Most women in nineteenth century China were considered no more than chattel. But the women in Namhoi, where Lai Yun Oi lived, were physically and economically independent. Footbinding was not widely practiced, and the women often supported themselves and their families by weaving baskets, raising mulberry, or working in the silk factories. Many women refused to marry, committing themselves to remaining single by going through a *sau-hai* ceremony of combing up their hair, sometimes joining sisterhoods for mutual support. Frequently, a wife who was unhappy left her husband's home. So when Yun Oi became widowed after only a year of marriage, she did not hesitate to strike out on her own.

At first she went to Canton to look for work. Then, in the late 1870s, she accompanied a fellow clan member to America. While the clansman went on to New York, Yun Oi chose to stay in San Francisco, where she worked as a *dai-kum*, bride escort. The duties of an escort began with combing the bride's girlish braids into a matronly bun and dressing her for the journey to the groom's home. She accompanied the bride in the wedding procession, carried her over the threshold, and helped her through the long day of rituals, from making obeisances to the parents and ancestors of the groom to the tea ceremony and banquet. Then she prepared the bride for her wedding night, leaving only when dismissed from the bridal chamber by the groom.

The scarcity of Chinese women in America—a total of 4,522 in 1900—meant Yun Oi could not support herself entirely as a *dai-kum*. She supplemented her income by doing needlework at home and providing hairdressing services for women in Chinatown. Living frugally, she invested her earnings in businesses in New York and San Francisco. When she retired just before the 1906 earthquake, Yun Oi was able to purchase several buildings for rentals and invest in a tailor shop in Canton.

Kindhearted and generous as well as capable, she returned to China with an adopted daughter, the child of a prostitute or some poor family in America. Then, after settling in a suburb of Canton, she adopted a son, and she was given the first-born daughter of a woman who had died in childbirth. This last girl, Dong Mui, became her favorite.

While in America, Yun Oi had maintained close ties with her sister, Mak Hing Oi, whose life as a married woman in Namhoi was a marked contrast to her own. Hing Oi, in addition to keeping house and raising three children, wove bamboo ware that was sold for cash. Her husband operated a hand loom at a small silk factory, where he boarded. Her father-in-law raised mulberry leaves and tended a fish pond on eight to ten *mus* (roughly one and a half acres) of rented land. Pooling their earnings, the family cleared several hundred dollars annually. But so marginal was this hard-earned self-sufficiency that a single blow could destroy it.

Disaster struck one wintry night after Hing Oi's father-in-law had prepared the fish pond for harvesting by lowering the water level. Unexpectedly, the temperature dipped below freezing. By dawn, all the fish were floating belly up. Dead fish had little market value, and their sale did not bring enough to pay the rent for the land or to repay the debts incurred at the beginning of the growing season. The shock killed the man, and Hing Oi's husband had to leave his job at the factory to take over the farming.

The subsistence economy of southern China was such that once a family was in debt, it was almost impossible for it to work its way back out unless a member went overseas and sent money home. Hing Oi's family would be no exception, so they sent their eldest son, sixteen-year-old Bing, to Singapore with a distant relative.

Going to work in Gold Mountain, as Yun Oi had done, would have been preferable. But she had entered America before the Exclusion Act passed in 1882. Now admission was possible only if one was a government official, merchant, student, teacher, visitor, or United States citizen. Since Exclusion also barred Chinese from becoming naturalized citizens, the only way to qualify for this latter category was through birth (either in the United States or as the offspring of a United States citizen) or by becoming a "paper son."

A slot for a paper son was created when an American citizen of Chinese descent falsely reported the birth of a child, usually a male, in China after a visit home. This slot would then be sold to an individual, who gave up his own family name in order to become a paper son eligible for entry to America. Before 1906, the number of paper sons was limited as there were so few Chinese

Americans. But after the earthquake and fire in San Francisco destroyed the city's immigration and birth records, thousands of Chinese were able to claim they were born in San Francisco and thus citizens by birth. Subsequently, the paper son ruse became one of the most widespread and popular means for circumventing Exclusion.

Shortly after Bing left for Singapore, this option became available to him through his aunt, Yun Oi. Years before, she had helped a cousin, Lai Poon, emigrate. This cousin, now a successful merchant, was willing to repay the favor by making Bing his paper son. Delighted, the family sent for Bing to come home and prepare for a new life in America.

Preparations for Bing to become Lai Poon's paper son had to be thorough, for all Chinese claims for admission to America were held suspect until identities could be verified through cross-examinations. These interrogations were designed to exclude rather than to admit, and applicants like Bing and witnesses like his paper father, Lai Poon, had to give identical answers to questions such as: How many times a year did you receive letters from your father? How did your father send you money to travel to the United States? Who lived in the third house in the second row of houses in your village? Where was the rice bin located?

Typically, the interrogations for applicant and witnesses lasted two or three days, and any lapse could mean deportation. Detailed "coaching books" (with all the necessary facts pertaining to family, home life, and native village) had to be compiled. Since the type of questions asked often depended on an inspector's whim, efforts to anticipate all possibilities meant these coaching books often ran to forty or more pages, all of which had to be carefully memorized. In the decade prior to Bing's attempt, there was an average of 560 deportations a year.

Preparations for Bing to become Lai Poon's paper son were meticulous and fraught with worry. Finally, on December 17, 1909, he boarded the *S.S. Siberia,* and after a month's voyage, sailed into San Francisco. Following standard procedure, Bing and the other Chinese passengers were immediately transferred to a dilapidated wooden shed at the Pacific Steamship Company Wharf.

The wait for a summons to appear for a hearing on their application for admission could take months, and as many as 400 to 500 people were crammed into the shed at a time. For years Chinese leaders had complained about the filthy, unsafe quarters, and Bing's arrival coincided with the opening of a new immigration station on Angel Island, in the middle of San Francisco Bay.

The location was intended to prevent Chinese immigrants from communicating with Chinese on the outside, to isolate immigrants with communicable diseases, and to prevent escape. On January 22, 1910, nine days after his arrival, Bing was transferred, along with more than 400 detainees, to the new station.

Men and women, including husbands and wives, were separated and not allowed to see or communicate with each other again until they were admitted into the country or deported. Guards stood outside the locked doors of the dormitories, and a fence surrounded the detention barracks to prevent escapes. No visitors were permitted, and all letters and gift packages were examined for coaching notes.

Processing began with a health examination: trachoma, hookworm, and liver fluke, among other diseases, were grounds for deportation. Bing passed this test and the interrogation two weeks later. On Monday, February 7, 1910, he was admitted to America as Lai Bing.

For the next half-dozen years, Bing worked as a general helper and then as a sewing machine operator in garment factories in San Francisco and Oakland. During World War I, he became an agricultural worker, harvesting apples in Sebastopol. After the war, he divided his time between agriculture and the garment trade, contracting for apple crops when in season and working in the sewing factories the balance of the year.

By the early 1920s he had earned enough to consider marriage, and he returned to China. While he had been away, his aunt, Yun Oi, had continued to help the family; one of Bing's first duties was to go to Canton to thank her. When she suggested her second adopted daughter, Dong Mui, as a bride for him, he agreed readily.

Yun Oi arranged the match because she wanted Dong Mui to have the opportunities America had offered her. But times had changed, and Dong Mui and her husband did not enjoy Yun Oi's success. When Bing had first come to America in the early 1900s, most of the sewing machine operators were men. Although Chinese workers were generally forced to accept lower wages than white workers in comparable jobs, labor guilds in the sewing industry had regulated the hours

When Japan attacked China in 1931, Chinese throughout the world sought ways to help defend their homeland. Money was raised and flying schools were set up in Oregon and California to train young Chinese Americans. American-born Arthur Chin (Chin Suey Tin) dropped out of high school to enroll in the first class in Portland, Oregon. After getting his license in August 1932, he sailed to China, where he became an ace fighter pilot for the National Air Force. (Courtesy Arthur T. Chin)

Laura Lai's commitment to the principles on which Mun Ching was founded came from the inequities she had observed as a child. Though remittances from her father had allowed her to grow up in luxury, she "saw other families not having enough to eat, not even going to school because they had to help grow rice or sweet potatoes as soon as they were old enough to do anything. . . . I wondered about it. I wondered why China was like that. Why did we have to live that way?" This photograph of Laura (in braids) was taken at one of Mun Ching's many outings. (Courtesy Him Mark Lai)

and working conditions and ensured uniform rate structures.

Due to guild members' traditional male chauvinism, however, women were not permitted to join, and this provided an opening for employers to weaken the guilds by hiring women. As more women entered the industry and men began to retire or find work elsewhere, the power of the guilds declined. Without them, working conditions and pay deteriorated, and attempts to replace the guilds with unions failed.

Bing and Dong Mui attempted to break free by opening a small garment store in Oakland. But with the onset of the Depression, it failed, and both wife and husband had to work in San Francisco's sewing factories in order to feed and clothe their growing family. By the time their eldest son, Him Mark, graduated from high school, their dreams of better opportunities had died. When Him Mark enrolled in college, paying his way by working part-time in a sewing factory for twenty-five cents an hour, Bing tried to discourage him by pointing out the Chinese American college graduates who could not find work in their fields because of discrimination.

The San Francisco shipyards, gearing up for World War II, were offering good money, and Bing urged his son to give up college for a full-time job in the shipyards. Him Mark ignored him. "So my father kept giving me hell for going to school, and I just went on," Him Mark said.

Nevertheless, he was enough of a realist to declare a major in engineering, though his interest was in history and the humanities. That way, even if discrimination prevented him from working as an engineer in his own country, America, he would be able to go and contribute his skills to his parents' homeland, China.

He was encouraged in this plan by his teachers at Chinese evening school, who passed on to their students their own bitterness over discrimination in America and China's oppression by the Japanese. "We got all the business about reconstructing China and some of us felt this as a mission," Him Mark recalled.

When Him Mark graduated from college in 1947, China was in the throes of civil war, but in America, World War II had opened up job opportunities previously closed to Chinese. Instead of going to China, he secured an engineering job in San Francisco. Still, engineering was never more than a means to make a living, and history remained Him Mark's passion.

His interest in China and his desire to contribute did not fade either. Growing up in San Francisco's Chinatown during the Depression, he was keenly aware of hardship, the exploitation of workers in and out of

Members of Mun Ching performed in traditional and Western-style dramas at recreational centers, schools, and parks all over the San Francisco Bay Area. In the Western-style production, Laura is the young woman with braids. (Courtesy Him Mark Lai)

Detention centers for Chinese immigrants were set up at different ports of entry. The processing—from the initial physical examination through to the final interrogation—was so terrifying that it left a legacy of fear and a mistrust of government in those who endured it. San Francisco's Angel Island, pictured here, was the Ellis Island of the West. (Courtesy National Archives)

According to one woman who attended elementary school in San Francisco in the 1930s, students were sometimes taken to Angel Island on field trips. "I remember landing at the pier and being taken through the detention center as if it were not people that we were seeing in the barracks. I was only a girl then, but I can still remember the depression in the demeanor of the detainees, my horror at the callous attitude of my teachers and classmates." (Courtesy Chinese Culture Foundation Collection, Asian American Studies Library, University of California at Berkeley)

Interrogations were long and rigorous. In one case where a twelve-year-old boy was denied entry, the federal court reversed the decision and admitted the boy on the grounds that anyone could make a mistake in eighty-seven pages of testimony. (Courtesy National Archives)

In 1946, Lai Bing and Dong Mui sent this family photograph back to relatives in Namhoi. When their son, Him Mark (center, rear), visited China thirty years later, he and his cousins used it to identify themselves to each other in a crowded hotel lobby. (Courtesy Him Mark Lai)

While working as an engineer, Him Mark directed the first major exhibit on the Chinese American experience, Chinese of America 1785–1980, *which toured the United States for several years. In 1985, the exhibit's sponsor, the Chinese Culture Foundation of San Francisco, donated it to China's Overseas Chinese Historical Society. Him Mark is seen here translating the exhibit's text from English into Chinese for the opening in Shanghai. (Courtesy Him Mark Lai)*

the community. He recognized that it was competition that forced down workers' salaries. Believing social change could only come about through collective effort, he joined Mun Ching, a club that emphasized mutual aid, group guidance, and collective educational and social activities.

The limited relaxation of immigration laws after World War II produced a brief influx of Chinese immigrants, and Mun Ching instituted tutorial, counseling, and remedial programs to help them. Among those Him Mark tutored was Laura Jung, who had recently arrived to join her father, a cook in San Francisco.

"My English was so bad I had to start out in the third grade even though I was sixteen," she explained. "After a few months, I was transferred to high school. When I turned twenty, I decided to finish all my requirements in half a year. That was the year I met Him Mark. He would help me with United States history and walk me home every night, so we got to know each other in the regular American way."

Laura's parents opposed their plans to marry. "They said it was because I was from Chungshan district and his parents were from Namhoi. So in Chinese geography it was far away. They said, 'Why are you marrying someone so far away?' And I said, 'He is not far away. He's on Jackson and we're on Montgomery.'" When they persisted, she told them firmly, "My mind is all made up. Whether it's now or two years later I'm going to marry him. I have decided." The day after Laura graduated, she and Him Mark were married at City Hall.

This was the period of the Korean War and the McCarthy assault against liberals and organizations like Mun Ching. Despite harassment by FBI agents, a core group of forty members, including Him Mark and Laura, persisted, publishing a biweekly newsletter and presenting cultural programs that included drama and music (such as the "Yellow River Cantata") from post-revolutionary China. But when the club lost its headquarters in 1959, it disbanded.

Suddenly without an outlet for his energies outside of work, Him Mark felt "mentally restless." Then, in 1965, he went to an exhibit by the Chinese Historical Society of America. The fledgling society's purpose—to document and analyze Chinese American society from a Chinese American perspective—reflected his own lifelong interest in the history of the United States and China. He decided to join.

Reclaiming the past gave Him Mark a new focus for his energies, and he threw himself into the work. "I was

At the turn of the century, the guilds controlling the garment industry were so powerful that nonmembers were not permitted to work in the same factories as guild members, and Lai Bing joined a guild soon after his arrival. (Courtesy Chinese Culture Foundation Collection, Asian American Studies Library, University of California at Berkeley)

San Francisco architect Philip Choy laughingly refers to himself as a victim of the romanticized West. On family vacations, he would track old stagecoach trails and visit ghost
towns. "You could see evidence of the Chinese everywhere, but
you never heard about the role they played in building the
West." So when Chinese for Affirmative Action persuaded a
local television station to commit air time for a history of the
Chinese in America, Choy worked enthusiastically with Him
Mark Lai and other community historians to produce Gam
Saan Haak, "Gold Mountain Guest." After four years in
production, the six-part series aired in 1976 with Choy as
host/narrator. He is seen here on location in California's Gold
Country. (Courtesy Philip Choy)

younger and more vigorous, and I spent every Saturday and Sunday at the library searching for materials," he recalled. On occasion he even climbed in and out of dumpsters in Chinatown to reclaim potential archival material carelessly thrown away. And, recognizing the importance of oral history, he interviewed old-timers, including his parents.

Many Chinese Americans, stirred by the Civil Rights Movement, became interested in their own communities and history during the 1960s. In 1968, Him Mark was asked to write articles on Chinese American history for *East/West News,* a bilingual community newspaper. This series became the basis for *A History of the Chinese in California: A Syllabus,* published by the Chinese Historical Society of America in 1969.

That same year, Third World students—recognizing the severe inequities in American university curriculums—led the first student strike for ethnic studies at San Francisco State College. As a result, the college invited Him Mark, still a practicing engineer, and Philip Choy, an architect-historian, to teach the first course in Chinese American history in the United States. Two years later, they distilled their lectures into *Outlines: History of the Chinese in America.*

Both the *Syllabus* and *Outlines* have become standard reference works in the field. Previous works relied on English-language sources. But as Him Mark noted, "To attain an in-depth understanding of Chinese American history, culture, and society, researchers must use source materials that originate within the Chinese community."

These materials—newspapers, biographies, letters, organizational publications, and literature—have been largely untapped because most researchers of Chinese American history, even those who are of Chinese descent, cannot read Chinese. Him Mark, utilizing his bilingual skills as well as bicultural understanding, has reclaimed for non-Chinese readers a wealth of information on the personal experiences and processes within Chinese American communities, community politics and relations with China, and Chinatown institutions. His ground-breaking research in China and America has provided the foundation for much subsequent work by historians as well as the inspiration for creative writers and artists.

Leaving engineering, Him Mark has embarked on a new career as archivist and consultant at the Asian American Studies Library at the University of California at Berkeley. He believes in the need to expand Chinese American Studies. "We must examine the role of Chinese in America more critically. It isn't enough to document and talk about contributions. We must go deeper, much deeper, in order to fully probe and understand the processes governing the development of Chinese American communities. We should also be willing to reveal the negative as well as the positive aspects of our people and history, even if it means treading on toes."

◈ Contemporaries ◈

Eleanor Wong (third from left in back row) and the Wong family
(Courtesy Eleanor Wong Telemaque)

Eleanor Wong Telemaque,
American-Born and Foreign

The town of Albert Lea, Minnesota, in the 1930s was a mix of Norwegians, Danes, Swedes, Germans, Scots, Irish, and the Wong family. Eleanor, the third of ten Wong children, felt special when her teacher called on her to write Chinese on the blackboard for the class. She liked dressing up in Chinese clothes to march in the town's parades—until she was laughed at for carrying one end of the banner "Sons and Daughters of Norway." Then she decided, "It's crazy to stay Chinese in Minnesota."

Like many of the town's residents, Eleanor's parents were first-generation immigrants. Her mother refused to learn English, and if any child dared speak it at home, she would take her broom and threaten to sweep them out of the house, even if it was snowing. She also made sure the family celebrated all the Chinese holidays and followed traditional Chinese religious practices.

Eleanor's father lectured the children repeatedly on the evils of British imperialism and the virtues of Dr. Sun Yat-sen. Always he would conclude with the pronouncement, "Never forget you are Chinese." Yet he was well aware of the need to promote good relations with the people who patronized his restaurant, the Canton. And when besieged by the town's ministers to send his children to Sunday school, he satisfied all the denominations represented in Albert Lea by sending each child to a different church.

Eleanor struggled to make a place for herself between her parents' demands for a Chinese daughter and the world outside her home. She wanted desperately to be "American, one hundred percent all-American." At the same time, she longed to meet other Chinese her own age.

All the Chinese restaurants in towns around Albert Lea closed on the same day so the families could gather and visit. But these gatherings could not satisfy Eleanor's need to escape the isolation of being a member of the only Chinese family in town. When she was fifteen, she persuaded her parents to let her go to school in Chicago.

"I hadn't graduated from high school," she recalled. "But the University of Chicago had a special program where students didn't have to go to class and age wasn't important. You read all the great books and took comprehensive exams."

"I always loved writing, but I thought there were no Chinese American writers," she explained. So she decided to study political science. She hoped her courses and the activities of the Chinese Student Christian Association, which she joined, would help answer some of her questions and prepare her for a career that would enable her to go to China.

What made the greatest immediate impact on her, however, was a newly published autobiography of a young Chinese American woman, *Fifth Chinese Daughter*. The author, Jade Snow Wong, had been born half a continent away in San Francisco and raised in a Chinatown, but Eleanor recognized Wong's struggles to reconcile the differences between her racial identity and the non-Chinese world. Reading the book, Eleanor realized for the first time that she was not alone in either her confusion or her aspiration. Other Chinese Americans felt the tug and pull of two cultures. Other Chinese Americans wrote.

Actually, several literary societies had formed in Chinatowns across America by the 1880s, and in the early 1900s literary groups began to publish their work. During the 1940s—the same period Eleanor was studying in Chicago—there were lively discussions in Chinatown journals on ethnicism and what constituted Chinese American writing. One writer, Wenquan, defined it as "ethnicism + Western democratic ideas," and he advised writers to "absorb American culture and penetrate deeply into the Chinatown community to experience its life and understand its problems." Another writer, Lingling, warned against the creation of borders or territories in literary expression, predicting that the separation of "Chinatown writing" from mainstream literature would "stifle, isolate, and trap us inside a cage." Yet separatism was inevitable because of language—all these works were in Chinese, which Eleanor and most Americans could not read.

In an attempt to meet the needs of second-generation Chinese Americans like Eleanor, two young San Franciscans, Thomas Chinn and Chingwah Lee, started a weekly, the *Chinese Digest*, in English. Limited funds restricted distribution, and subscription and sales never exceeded 500, but letters to the editor during its five years of publication indicate the weekly did reach readers

Some Chinese parents focus on their children's "American" identity. Shawn Wong's parents, post-World War II immigrants from Taiwan (and no relation to Eleanor Wong), placed so much emphasis on their son's "American" identity that China's Chinese were nearly alien to him. When his father was working in Taiwan as a civilian engineer for the United States Navy, Wong, in the second grade, had to be placed in an American school (from which the Taiwanese were excluded). "Here I was," Wong recalled, "in the middle of Nationalist China, going to an all-white school because I couldn't speak Chinese." Though his first novel. Homebase, *was published by Ishmael Reed to critical acclaim, he now finds the manuscript of his second novel rejected by publishers with such comments as "English is clearly your second language." (Courtesy Shawn Wong)*

*Shawn Wong, who races cars professionally when he is not writing or teaching, said, "I like the fact that {in racing} you win or lose in a few seconds. It's settled, it's over. There's no middle ground." He is seen here with some of his many trophies. (Courtesy Natalie Fobes/*Seattle Times*)*

in Seattle, Hawaii, New Mexico, and the East Coast. Eleanor and other Chinese Americans living in remote areas generally did not know of its existence, however.

Living in Chicago made Eleanor realize just how sheltered her life had been in Albert Lea. Blacks had come through the little town only occasionally. She had heard the waitresses at the family's restaurant complain, "We got a black one," but they did not resist when her father said, "You have to serve them." She had experienced some name-calling herself but had never taken it to heart, equating "Chinky Chinky Chinaman" with her mother's usual conversational reference to whites as *bak gwai,* white devils. Observing blatant discrimination for the first time in Chicago, Eleanor signed a membership card for the American Youth for Democracy and picketed Montgomery Ward for refusing to hire blacks.

"Then the revolution in China took place. I was homesick for my family, and when I realized China was closed to Americans and I wouldn't be able to go, I went back to Minnesota and studied journalism at the State University." She did not realize that the revolution and China's subsequent participation in the Korean War would unleash a decade of anti-Communist hysteria in the United States that would profoundly affect her father and herself and, indeed, all Americans, especially those of Chinese descent.

According to J. Edgar Hoover, the head of the FBI, all Chinese in America were "susceptible to recruitment [by Chinese Communists] through ethnic ties or hostage situations because of relatives in Communist China." These accusations were similar to the ones that had led to the internment of Japanese Americans during World War II. In fact, with passage of Title II of the Internal Security Emergency Act (passed over President Truman's veto) in 1950, Chinese Americans were threatened with the possibility of internment in the same camps that had held the Japanese Americans.

In 1955, after Everett F. Drumright, United States Consul in Hong Kong, encouraged suspicion of Chinese Americans by claiming that many were illegal aliens and that some of the illegals were possible Communist agents, there was talk of mass persecutions and deportations. The U.S. Department of Justice, along with the Chinese Six Companies and other benevolent associations, responded by devising the Confession Program. Chinese who had falsely claimed American citizenship were encouraged to confess their true identities, with the promise of "maximum relief possible under existing laws and regulations." Determination of "maximum relief," however, was up to the Justice Department, and not only could the "confessee" be prosecuted, but so could relatives, friends, and acquaintances.

First-generation immigrant parents often stress their American-born children's "Chinese" identity. Rosemarie Fay Loomis grew up in Rochester, New York, but she spent every summer in New York's Chinatown. "Other children got to go to camp. But my father sent me to live with a Chinese family so I could learn to speak Chinese. It was like eating spinach—something you have to do because it's good for you. But I'm still close to that family and their daughter is like a sister to me." (Courtesy Rosemarie Fay Loomis)

To coerce confessions, Chinese and Chinese Americans were frequently stopped on the streets, questioned, and required to produce documents that proved their legal status. Fear swept through Chinatowns all across America. In Chicago, where Eleanor's parents had moved, her father, Wong Sang, became one of thousands summoned for interrogation.

Sang, like many other Chinese Americans, was an illegal alien. During the six decades of Exclusion, however, there had been no way for the majority of Chinese to emigrate to America legally—and Exclusion was so obviously unfair that Sang and others had no compunction about finding ways to circumvent the law.

As a child, Eleanor had observed how their European neighbors only had to save for a relative's passage, whereas for the Wongs' relatives, passage was not enough: there also had to be money for false papers. Not surprisingly, her mother came to consider Exclusion no more than a challenge to her ingenuity. When

The hero in Eleanor Wong Telemaque's novel It's Crazy to Stay Chinese in Minnesota *was inspired by her first boyfriend, John Yuen, pictured above. (Courtesy Eleanor Wong Telemaque)*

As an experiment, playwright Frank Chin asked students at San Francisco State University to fold a piece of paper in half and list all their "American" qualities on one side and their "Chinese" qualities on the other. "Everything that was interesting, adventurous, original, creative, fun, sexy, daring, artistic, was American. Everything old-fashioned, inhibiting, restraining, dull, repressive, uncreative, stultifying, was Chinese," he recalled. "It's because the title 'Chinese American,' the cliché 'blending East and West,' encourages you to say, 'Well, what are my Chinese parts? What are my American parts?' And what you break down, you break down according to the lines of stereotype. It's something conditioned into you that you don't even realize. It's self-contempt." (Courtesy Connie Young Yu)

she noticed that white people generally thought all Chinese looked alike, she daringly smuggled several relatives across the Minnesota-Canadian border by driving into Canada with one set of passengers and returning with another.

Even after the Exclusion Act was repealed in 1943, the number of Chinese immigrants permitted each year was so small (105) that Chinese Americans who wanted to reunite their families still had to be resourceful. After passage of the 1945 War Brides Act (allowing foreign wives of American servicemen to enter America), Eleanor's mother was always on the lookout for unmarried veterans; all young Chinese males who stopped to eat at the Canton when passing through Albert Lea were interrogated by her on their marital status.

Eleanor's father had been born in Toishan and had emigrated as a "paper son," an American born in Redlands, California. The implication that he might be a Communist could not have been further from the truth, for Sang was a dedicated supporter of Chiang Kai-shek, leader of the Kuomintang, the party America had supported in China's civil war.

Like many other Chinese Americans, Sang had helped raise thousands of dollars for the Kuomintang's fight against the Communists. Chinatown newspapers, language schools, and traditional organizations, such as the Chinese Consolidated Benevolent Association, also took a strong anti-Communist stand, continuing to support the Kuomintang in Taiwan long after its defeat in China. Chinatown organizations sympathetic to the Kuomintang even encouraged the anti-Communist campaign at its inception, eliminating opponents by denouncing them to the Immigration Office as Communists and working with the Justice Department during the 1950s to convict the editors of a left-wing paper, the *China Daily News,* for violating the Trading with the Enemy Act. But in the maelstrom of the witch-hunt that they—at least in part—helped launch, all Chinese Americans became suspect, and Sang could not avoid interrogation.

"Confess," the officers told him.

Fully aware that any confession would necessitate informing on others, Sang answered, "I born Redlands, California."

"Confess," the officers insisted.

"I born Redlands, California," he repeated.

Eleanor accompanied her father and she could clearly see his fear. Yet he never swerved from "I born Redlands, California" despite hours of intense grilling. "That was the first time I recognized my father's courage," Eleanor said, "and the first time I understood the difficulties of survival for a Chinese in America." Thinking of herself only as an American, however, she never imagined for a moment that she, too, would come under suspicion.

She was working in Washington, D.C., for the State Department in 1956 and had applied for a position at Voice of America. "Anyone who applied to work there was automatically investigated and I was hauled before the Department of State's Loyalty Board and accused of being a Communist sympathizer. The American Youth for Democracy that I had joined in Chicago was apparently considered a 'commie front.' Also, while attending the University of Minnesota, I lived at the International Student House, and I was supposed to have said that 'Communism might be good for China.'" Defended by Theodore C. Sorenson, the brother of a for-

mer college roommate, Eleanor was cleared of the charges.

Other Chinese Americans, like Maurice Chuck, a private in the United States Army, were not so fortunate. He was court-martialed for joining the Chinese American Democratic Youth League and speaking out in favor of diplomatic ties between China and the United States. "They gave me an undesirable discharge and took my belongings, my diary, even the manuscript of an unfinished novel I was writing."

The effects of the "Red Hunt" were far reaching. People who confessed subjected those they implicated to interrogations, which in turn led to more betrayals. Inside Chinatowns, suspicion and rumors flourished. Dissent vanished. A few embittered Chinese Americans voluntarily left the United States for China. The vast majority remained, with some fighting deportation in the courts for as many as seventeen years.

Gradually, with the normalization of relations between China and America in the 1970s, the perception that Americans of Chinese descent were aliens, enemy aliens, receded. Yet the impression that they are still not quite "one hundred percent American" lingers.

When Eleanor submitted the manuscript of her semi-autobiographical novel *It's Crazy to Stay Chinese in Minnesota* to publishers, she was asked to change the principal male character from Chinese to white so that the love relationship would be Chinese-white. Eleanor refused. It wasn't that she opposed interracial relationships. The young man who had inspired the character in the book had married a white woman. Eleanor's own husband, Maurice Telemaque, is Haitian. What she objected to was the publisher's implication that a Chinese American male was unacceptable as a hero. Finally, Thomas Nelson Inc. accepted Eleanor's book as she had written it, and it was published in 1978.

Now a full-time writer living in New York City, she was recently honored with the Manhattan Borough President's Award for Excellence in the Arts in the field of prose literature. She is currently completing a novel, *American Son.*

Harry Lee; his wife, Lai; and daughter, Cynthia
(Courtesy Harry Lee)

Harry Lee,
Chinese Cowboy

In 1975, when Harry Lee ran for Sheriff of Jefferson Parish just outside of New Orleans, the political support he expected did not materialize. Withdrawing from the race, he took an appointment as Parish Attorney. Four years later, he resigned the post and again ran for Sheriff. "But I didn't have a Chinaman's chance to win," he recalled.

Harry had not always had political aspirations. At his father's urging, he had majored in petroleum engineering in college. Then, when he could not pass the math and physics courses required, he transferred to geology. The decision was pragmatic: he had built up a lot of geology credits. But his counselor told him he would recommend Harry for any job in the country—except geologist. "He said I'd make a helluva salesman because I liked to be around people. I guess that was something I always knew but didn't realize until he told me."

Still unclear about a career, Harry enlisted in the Air Force as a second lieutenant. When he completed his tour, he joined his father and eight siblings at the family's newly opened restaurant, House of Lee, working as manager. While a member and then president of the local chapter of the Louisiana Restaurant Association, he worked on promoting the full accommodation of black patrons and on a minimum wage bill. Thinking a knowledge of the law would be helpful, he enrolled in law school.

His interest in politics awakened, he began serving as a volunteer assistant and confidant to Louisiana Congressman Hale Boggs. Boggs, the majority leader of the House of Representatives, wielded considerable influence. But as Harry observed, "In the legislature you can't do anything on your own. Even as a member of the local (seven-person) council, I could come up with an idea that could save the Parish twenty million dollars, but if I couldn't convince three others that it would work, it'd go down the tubes."

At the urging of Boggs, Harry sought and was appointed to the position of Federal Magistrate by the District Court Judge. His jurisdiction covered about half the state of Louisiana. "The job was like a judge's," Harry explained, "and I stayed five years. But I found it confining. Every day was the same thing. It just wasn't fun."

He resigned to run for Sheriff, the third most important job in Louisiana, with only the Governor and the Mayor of New Orleans enjoying more power. "The Sheriff is answerable only to the voters," Harry explains. "He's the complete boss." As such he can hire and fire, punish and reward as he sees fit—the power and the responsibility not unlike that of the Chinese head man for nineteenth century work gangs.

Born in 1932, Harry was too young to know about them. But he had seen and admired the authority his father, Lee Bing, wielded. Bing, only six when he had crossed an ocean and half a continent to join his own father in New Orleans, had attended American schools and had practically been raised by the mother of one of his American schoolmates. Fluent in English and comfortable with Western manners and customs, he interpreted for the United States Immigration Service (in addition to running a laundry), traveling throughout Louisiana, Mississippi, and Arkansas.

Historically, Chinese who served as interpreters for their countrymen often became advocates for their interests, and Bing became a leader for the Chinese community in New Orleans. Anyone with a problem went to him for help; Bing was trusted absolutely. "At election time he would drive around town and tell everyone [other Chinese] how he was voting, and they would vote the same way," Harry recalled.

By the time Harry ran for office, Chinese American voters were far more sophisticated. But they were (and are still) underrepresented in elected offices. According to Harry, "Chinese Americans may have respect for government, but they don't participate in it much."

Lingering fears from the long years of Exclusion are, in part, responsible for this lack of participation. "Because of the discrimination [Chinese Americans have] faced, they've never trusted government or politicians and shied away from politics," explained California's Secretary of State, March Fong Eu. "[But] they are realizing that they must participate if they are going to have any influence."

Another effect of Exclusion is the paucity of Chinese Americans. Though they are one of the fastest growing minorities in the country, they number less than two million. Of these, many are new immigrants who are not yet qualified to become citizens or who avoid politics because they have come from countries where political involvement is dangerous. In order to make any kind of impact, Chinese Americans would have to vote in a block. Just because they share a common ethnicity, however, does not mean they share a common ancestry or beliefs: American-born Chinese have different goals from immigrants who, coming from different parts of China, Asia, and South America, are also diverse in culture, language, and politics.

Even where Chinese Americans have unified, the results have been disappointing. "Nationally [Chinese Americans] rank only behind Jews in financial support of the Democratic party," said San Francisco Municipal Court Judge Lillian Sing. "But as far as a return goes, the results are minimal."

The number of Chinese Americans in Jefferson Parish is insignificant. As in other parts of the country, they are an incohesive mix of American-born Chinese and immigrants from Taiwan, China, and Hong Kong. Harry claims that being of Chinese ancestry has helped rather than hurt his career in the predominantly white, middle-class parish. "If I'm one of fifty people at a party, the other forty-nine will remember a big Chinaman was there." Indeed, the greatest hurdle he had to overcome in his campaign for Sheriff was his lack of recognition by the general electorate.

What finally gave him the recognition he needed was a commercial that showed Harry in cowboy boots, western shirt, jeans, and a cowboy hat, walking on a levee with his wife and daughter. Within two days, he was a celebrity. "How many six-foot-tall, 260-pound Chinamen do they have around who wear a cowboy hat?" he laughed. "Everywhere I'd go people would come up and ask me where my hat was. It got to be a part of me."

The image of Harry as a Chinese cowboy won him the election against a sixteen-year incumbent. The Sheriff's office is responsible for collecting taxes as well as law enforcement, and Harry controls a staff of 1,300 and a budget of thirty million dollars. "It's basically a lot of administrative work, organization, public relations, and fund raising," he explained.

One of the first major changes Harry made after his election was to make himself more accessible to his employees and the public than his predecessor had been. He takes an active role in investigations, and, in order to keep in touch with what is going on at a grassroots level, he makes time to cruise the parish in a police car "with a few of the guys" and to have coffee and doughnuts with a couple of deputies around eleven every night.

This means putting in twelve- to sixteen-hour days "not out of necessity but because I love the work." Besides, Harry is used to long hours. When he decided to go to law school while managing House of Lee, his father gave him permission so long as he did it on his own time. "I'd go to class early in the morning, get to the restaurant at one in the afternoon, and work until one in the morning, six days a week." While working for Congressman Boggs as a volunteer, Harry was also running his own law practice. During his tenure as a Federal Magistrate, he put in a lot of extra work as president of the Council of United States Magistrates. While working as Parish Attorney, he served on the Federal Advisory Board for Immigration. And throughout, he has continued to serve in the Air Force Reserves. "I'm an overachiever," he said. "I always want to be doing something."

The walls of Harry's offices are covered with awards from the Paralyzed Veterans of America, YMCA, Delta Area Democrats, and other organizations. An affable, outgoing man, he expresses genuine interest in and concern for the "little guy." When a fire on December 24, 1983, burned out sixteen low-income families, Harry galvanized the Sheriff's Department into action, arranging hotel accommodations, emergency supplies, and Christmas dinner.

The day after Christmas, he and his deputies took the fifty-eight fire victims shopping, buying each person a jacket or coat, a pair of shoes, three pairs of socks, three sets of underwear, two pants or skirts, and two shirts or blouses. Five thousand dollars of the $8,000 bill was covered in donations, and Harry personally paid the balance. Yet, according to a radio broadcast, "[Lee] shuns personal credit for any of this. 'These people needed help,' he said, 'so it was just a good community effort.'"

For Harry, who can make a party out of what other people consider work, public appearances—even four or five in a row—are no chore. "I like people," he said simply, "and people enjoy seeing me and being with me."

Certainly they liked Harry well enough to re-elect him in 1984. But a third term seemed in jeopardy after his announcement in December 1986 that blacks in mostly white neighborhoods would be stopped and questioned. Acknowledging that singling out blacks was a harsh policy, he claimed such a measure was necessary in order to stop the rash of crimes in which robbers were following Christmas shoppers to their homes and mugging them in their driveways. He also presented statistics indicating that seventy-nine percent

Since New Orleans was a port of entry for immigrants, the New Orleans newspapers (up to the repeal of Exclusion) frequently reported on Chinese immigration problems—from the capture of suspected smugglers and illegals to the deportation of a World War I veteran who had lived in the country for thirty-two years. The papers also reported protests by Chinese. One protest came from Mrs. John Fong, the wife of one of New Orleans' largest importers of Chinese goods, who told how her brother-in-law was deported three times before finally being admitted. "I hope that some day Chinese will be admitted to this country as are the natives of other countries," she concluded. That was 1911. When Harry Lee was serving on the Federal Advisory Board for Immigration (from 1976 to 1979), he was still trying to achieve this goal by pushing for an increase in the restrictive quota for Chinese from Hong Kong. (Courtesy Historic New Orleans Collection, Museum/Research Center)

When the director of the New Orleans Summer Pops told Harry they were losing money, he organized a benefit that raised over $25,000 in a single night of country-western music. Opening the act by dancing a spirited Cotton-Eyed Joe with Lai, Harry went on to sing six songs with the Hank Williams Original Drifting Cowboys Band. (Courtesy Harry Lee)

Charges of racism are explosive; at the same time they can be hard to prove. In 1982, Vincent Chin, a Chinese American draftsman, got into a name-calling altercation at a Detroit nightclub with Ronald Ebens and Michael Nitz, two unemployed auto workers who mistook him for a Japanese. Outside the club, he was chased down by the two men and so severely beaten with a baseball bat that he died of his injuries four days later. Ebens and Nitz were fined $3,780 and given three years' probation. When Asian American activists protested, the Justice Department brought Ebens to trial in federal court on the charge that he violated Chin's civil rights by attacking Chin because of his race. Found guilty, Ebens' conviction was overturned on a technicality, and the jury in a retrial—unconvinced that "racial intent" had prompted the murder—acquitted him. (Courtesy East/West News)

of the robberies in the previous month had been committed by blacks.

Though advised to carry out the policy in secrecy, Harry insisted it was his duty to inform the public of the Department's actions. "I'm interested in getting things done, and I'm willing to take the rap or credit," he said.

It was not the first time he had made a controversial statement. His use of the terms *Chinaman* and *Oriental*, for example, is offensive to many. And during the Bakke reverse discrimination case, he told the Organization of Chinese Americans that he was against quotas. "Since quotas are usually set up by the percentage of the population and the Chinese population is small, they will lose out. Orientals in general, and Chinese in particular, can do better competing for slots than having quotas set aside for them." But his order to stop blacks without probable cause was a violation of civil rights, and it touched off a fire storm of protests and demands for his resignation that did not cease when he revoked the order the following day.

With a constituency that is twelve percent black and eighty-five percent white, there were inevitably some residents of the parish who called him a hero. To Harry, this praise was more disturbing than the criticism. "It distresses me greatly that I have been characterized as a bigot and racist because I know in my heart how it feels to be treated differently."

He reminded the public of his civil rights record. As president of the New Orleans Chapter of the Louisiana Restaurant Association, he had been primarily responsible for the peaceful integration of New Orleans' restaurants. While United States Magistrate, he had granted more habeas corpus relief—most of it for civil rights violations—than any other magistrate in the United States. Shortly after becoming Sheriff, he had ordered the Junior Deputy camps integrated. And during his tenure, he has increased the number of black employees appreciably and terminated white officers for drawing their weapons on black citizens.

Successfully riding out the furor, Harry was re-elected in 1987. "I want to be around another twenty years," he said. "I can do a lot of good things here."

In 1983, Harry was awarded the AMVETS (American Veterans of World War II, Korea, and Vietnam) Silver Helmet Award, which is presented annually to "men and women who have rendered services of a distinguished nature to veterans, American communities, the nation, and the world at large." The inscription reads, "Presented to Mr. Harry Lee, Sheriff, Parish of Jefferson, Louisiana, in grateful recognition of unselfish promotion of patriotic interests, activities and values, thus providing an inspiring example of the kind of American citizenship that made this nation great." (Courtesy Harry Lee)

Adrienne Telemaque
(Courtesy Adrienne Telemaque)

Adrienne Telemaque
versus Suzie Wong

New York theatre auditions are known as cattle calls. Dozens of actors and actresses compete for the few available jobs in a process that is demeaning to all and especially difficult for ethnic minorities. Actress Adrienne Telemaque, who is of mixed Haitian and Chinese ancestry, has found that "At calls for black actresses I'm not 'black' enough and at Asian calls I'm not 'Asian' enough."

That some people have problems with her ethnicity is nothing new for Adrienne. Growing up in an Irish-Catholic and German neighborhood of Manhattan in the 1960s, she had attended a parochial school where the nuns disapproved of her because she is half black. Since her father, a devout Catholic, refused to take her out of the school, her mother—in an attempt to counteract the negativism Adrienne had to confront daily—enrolled the girl, then only six, in ballet classes.

"I took to it from the start because I liked the kids," Adrienne recalled. "They were from public school, and there were Jews and other mixed kids, so I felt comfortable there." With classes from four to five thirty every afternoon and frequent performances on nights and weekends, ballet became her life. When she was twelve years old, she began to take it seriously, and she worked at completing high school early so she could get into a company by the time she was fifteen.

The only break was summers with her paternal grandparents in Haiti. Like many immigrants, her father's ties to family and friends in the "old country" are still strong. Before starting school, Adrienne had lived in Haiti for a full year, and she grew up speaking French and Creole as well as English. "I had tons of cousins here in New York as well as Haiti, so I was always surrounded by the culture, and there was a lot of love. It was great."

Her mother [see Chapter Thirteen] and her maternal aunts and uncles, who had grown up in Minnesota, were "very American." She rarely saw her maternal grandparents in Chicago. "It wasn't until I joined the San Francisco Ballet Company when I was sixteen that I learned about Chinese culture," Adrienne said. "I lived with my uncle's family, and his wife, who is from Taiwan, taught me."

Adrienne's husband, Philip Nash, is of Japanese and Irish descent, and she has learned about those cultures as well. "My friends are from every culture. Choosing just one or two would be too isolating." In fact, she quit ballet in her early twenties because "as part of a corps de ballet, you have to be like everyone else. You can't be an individual." She has since discovered that the theatrical world demands its own uniformity through its adherence to age-old stereotypes.

Historically, Chinatowns and their inhabitants have been portrayed in the media as exotic but sinister. Today, Fu Manchu villains have been updated to modern-day gangsters, while dragon ladies and China dolls have not changed at all. "Good" Asian males have gone from physical laborers (cooks, houseboys, and laundrymen) to technical laborers (laboratory technicians and businessmen). And "good" Asian women, like these emasculated men, are quiet and passive, even meek. These are the images casting directors have in mind at auditions, and they are so powerful that Chinese American actors and actresses sometimes become doubtful about who they are, affecting phony accents and using eyebrow pencils to make their eyes more slanted.

For a long time, Adrienne resisted catering to the stereotype. "Finally, I did get myself a Suzie Wong wig," she said. "I hated doing it. But it's what they want. After buying the wig, I got the first job I went out for."

There are those who condemn actors and actresses for accepting such casting, for the damage caused by stereotypic images can be far reaching. Many Chinese Americans see a connection between the dehumanization of Asians in Rambo-type movies and the rise in anti-Asian violence. And for some Chinese Americans, the result of seeing only negative images of themselves in the media is self-hate.

One man said, "I remember rushing home from school one afternoon—I was eleven or twelve years old—and desperately staring at the bathroom mirror and praying to God my face would miraculously turn Caucasian. . . . Only fear of pain and death kept me from committing suicide." Neither could he admit to his white schoolmates that his father was a laundryman.

Adrienne considers herself "half-Chinese and half-Haitian, equal parts of my parents {Eleanor Wong and Maurice Telemaque, above}. But my mother thinks of herself as American rather than Chinese, and my father feels more Latin than American." (Courtesy Eleanor Wong Telemaque)

Adrienne with and without her Suzie Wong wig. (Courtesy Adrienne Telemaque)

"I insisted that my friends not walk me home because I did not want them to know what my father did. If they asked, I could never bring myself to tell the truth. 'He's a guard downtown,' I would say. He is this, he is that, anything but a laundryman."

So pervasive is stereotyping that even when progress is ostensibly made, such as the hiring of Chinese American anchors on television news programs, only "exotic" women have been hired, not one "unattractive" man. "People think Asians have done so well," said San Francisco television anchor Emerald Yeh, "but how can you say that if one entire gender group is hardly visible?"

Similarly, Chinese American men find themselves readily hired by large corporations but bypassed for promotion to managerial positions because of the perception that they are quiet and passive, therefore weak and less capable of handling people—or, as David Lam, chief executive officer of a thriving Silicon Valley company, puts it, "workhorses and not racehorses."

Chinese American actors and actresses are also trapped by the stereotypes they are forced to play. As one actor said in self-defense, "If you have not worked for many months or years, it becomes very difficult to make any artistic choices when you are hungry."

What sometimes drives Adrienne to compromise in taking a role is not the need for money so much as her desire to work in her preferred career as actress, dancer, and singer. While with the San Francisco Ballet, she had torn a hamstring in the back of her knee. The physical therapist had been very supportive, and when Adrienne quit ballet, she chose to earn a degree and license in physical therapy. "The money is good. But I want to just do theatre," she said. "I've danced with a small modern company, been in a summer stock tour of *King and I* in New England, and worked dinner theatre." Most recently, she played the featured role of Liat in New York City Opera's revival of *South Pacific*.

She was fortunate to be cast in these shows, for roles calling for blacks or Asians are not only stereotypic but scarce. And while few directors or producers today would cast a white in a distinctly black role, they do not appear to have the same qualms about casting whites in yellow face. In an interview in the 1970s, Roland Winters, who played the lead in a number of Charlie Chan films, said, "If you want to cast a homosexual in a show, and you get a homosexual, it'll be awful. It won't be funny. If you get a man, a normal man, playing a homosexual, it's funny." Casting Asians in Asian roles would be similarly inappropriate, he claimed, though "militant minorities" would probably disagree.

American-born artist and writer Deng Ming Dao believes, "Americans don't respect Third World men. They don't think we can be heroic or gentle or handsome or good. Even though I am published and have my work in museum collections, it doesn't seem to be enough. At publishing parties or museum receptions, I'm often patronized by people who say, 'Oh, your English is very good,' or 'I know this lovely Chinese restaurant,' and I want to ask, 'What do I have to do to get taken seriously and treated with respect?'" (Courtesy Deng Ming Dao. Photograph by Kenneth Ma)

Acts like "The Whoopee Review" were popular during vaudeville's heyday because Chinese American performers were considered a novelty by the predominantly white audiences. At one point there was even a touring Chinese black-faced minstrel troupe, the brainchild of a San Francisco missionary, Charles Shepherd. (Courtesy Performing Arts Research Center, the New York Public Library at Lincoln Center)

Part of the difficulty in fighting stereotypes is that not everyone agrees on what is stereotypic. When Flower Drum Song *became a smash hit on Broadway in the 1950s, critics hailed it as a "striking and healthy change" in American attitudes toward the Chinese. Today, opinion is divided between Chinese Americans who still find it a realistic and touching love story and those who consider it an offensive distortion of Chinatown life. (Courtesy Museum of Modern Art)*

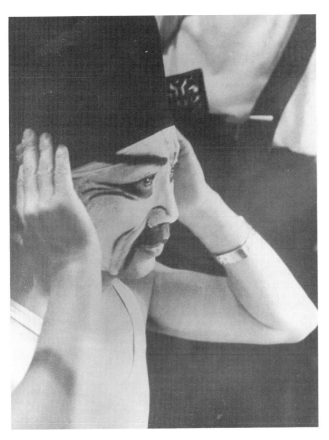

Some Chinese Americans have compromised by working during the day in "drudge" jobs and practicing their art at night. During the 1950s and 1960s, Steven Shimin Young, an accountant in Manhattan, performed with the Yeh Yu (After Work) Chinese Opera Association. "He was never happy at work, and he had a hard time keeping a job," his daughter, Rebecca Young, recalled. "But he was such a popular performer that the minute he walked on stage the whole audience would go wild with applause." (Courtesy Rebecca Young)

The daughter of a Korean father and Chinese mother, filmmaker Christine Choy grew up in Shanghai, moving to Korea for high school and then to America for college. Her first major film effort was with a black woman, Susan Robeson. Together they examined the brutality and overcrowding at Attica State Prison, and the result, Teach Our Children, won first prize at the International Black Film Festival in 1974. Choy, however, was not permitted to receive the award with Robeson because she was not black. Choy said, "I've come to realize that substance, not form, is what matters—in film and in life. It doesn't matter how old you are, what color you are, or who you live with. These are only forms." (Courtesy Christine Choy)

Others, like Dr. Tony Eng, have found satisfaction in both their careers and avocations. A successful orthopedic surgeon, Eng is also an enthusiastic member of a New Jersey barbershop chorus that sings in competitions all over the country. (Courtesy Dr. Tony Eng)

The burden of being an artist in a hostile environment can become overwhelming. During the 1930s and 1940s, Yun Gee was a rising modernist painter, in the company of Georgia O'Keeffe. His primary subjects were ordinary human beings observed in the day-to-day routine of life, and his work—a unique synthesis of East and West—was exhibited in several important New York galleries. Nevertheless, the constant struggle for recognition as an artist rather than "an Oriental from Chinatown" caused him to suffer a breakdown from which he never fully recovered. (Courtesy Helen Gee)

Radio has provided an outlet for the talents of some Chinese Americans. During the 1940s, actress Barbara Jane Wong was a professional voice for many "little girl" parts. Dr. Herb Wong has been a jazz radio broadcaster for over twenty-seven years. Listeners often express amazement that the eloquent voice on his show Jazz Prospectus belongs to an Asian. "We think we have to categorize, to classify everything," he said. "But we don't have to." (Courtesy Library of Congress)

As Winters predicted, Asian Americans did complain when a new Charlie Chan movie was made with a white actor playing the lead. But the film failed because of poor reviews rather than the protests, which were spearheaded in the San Francisco Bay Area by Forrest Gok. "We don't have the numbers or the networking that the National Association for the Advancement of Colored People has to be really effective," he explained.

So the practice of white actors playing Asian roles continues. Film producers defend their decisions on the grounds that they must have bankable stars or that Asian American actors lack the necessary experience. Regional theatres, like the Asolo in Sarasota, Florida, maintain that they need actors who can perform in Japanese plays, such as *Rashomon,* as well as the Western shows that more commonly rotate in repertory, such as *The Importance of Being Earnest.*

When Actors Equity complained about the all-white cast at Asolo, John Ulmer, the artistic director, responded, "Casting Asian Americans in *The Importance of Being Earnest* would be a denial of the script. Why wasn't it a denial, then, to cast whites in *Rashomon?* Because our director felt it was not a bizarre Oriental play, but a universal one."

It is exactly this attitude—that Asians are somehow not normal—that some Chinese Americans in the media have been attempting to combat. "There have to be movies that deal with Chinese as real people, people who eat McDonald's hamburgers and go through day-to-day things just like you and me," said filmmaker Wayne Wang.

Also attempting to present the Asian American point of view to the public are nonprofit theatre companies such as the Pan Asian Repertory in New York. Adrienne became involved with them when they needed dancers for an Asian American version of *West Side Story* and then a Filipino American play, *State Without Grace.* "It felt so good to be working with other Asian Americans. It was like being with another mixed person. They understood the pleasures and the problems without any need to explain."

Such opportunities are rare, however, and Adrienne admitted, "Mostly it's my work as a therapist that pays the rent." And when she *is* offered commercial theatrical work, there is often little pleasure. Rather, she must make complex decisions about whether to take the role.

After much soul searching, Adrienne reluctantly accepted the part of a black woman in a South African company's commercial to be shown in Africa. "Everything about the job was right except I was doing it for the wrong people," she said. "I'm against apartheid in South Africa, but I'm a victim too. I can't get work in America."

Pamela Wong (left) planting rice in Bak Sa Village, China
(Courtesy Pamela Wong)

Pamela Wong
and Her Search for Roots

Pamela Wong was stooped over the muddy water of a paddy field planting rice when she heard giggling. Looking up, her eyes met the curious stares of two girls on a bicycle that was swerving toward the edge of the road. Before she could call out a warning, the bicycle smashed into a tree, throwing the girls into the mud. Watching them scramble to their feet, retrieve their bicycle, and scurry away, Pamela laughed: it served them right for staring!

Growing up in Portland, Oregon, in the 1960s, she had never thought much about being different. Her mother's family was of European and French Canadian ancestry, and Pamela knew they had disapproved of her mother's marriage to a Chinese American. But that side of the family lived in Virginia and she rarely saw them. Her Chinese grandparents lived nearby, and she sensed that they subtly favored their one child who had married a Chinese. But the Portland Chinese community accepted her parents' marriage without question, and Pamela had never been singled out for comment regarding her ancestry either in or out of Chinatown.

In China, however, she was a novelty. The family she was living with in Bak Sa Village, Toishan, introduced her to everyone not as Wong Mei Qin (Pamela's Chinese name) but as *mei gok nui*, American girl. She was discussed openly and at length by strangers and friends alike. "Oh, what pretty light skin," people would remark; then they would ask, "Why do you look a little Chinese?"

The people were friendly, and she realized that the stares and talk were not prompted by any animosity. "But I never got used to it," she admitted. Nevertheless, Pamela has no regrets about her decision to "go back" to her grandfather's village.

The idea had come to her in college. Before that—though her father had served as president of the Chinese Consolidated Benevolent Association in Portland and the family regularly attended Chinese functions—Pamela had felt no more of a connection with China than she did with Europe. But during her sophomore year at Lewis and Clark College, she signed up for Beginning Chinese. The professor, Lu Yutai, was from China. Meeting him, listening to him talk, and learning the language made the country real; Pamela became "hooked on going to China."

She knew that since Nixon's visit to China in 1972, many Americans of Chinese ancestry had "gone back" on tours and that it was possible to take a few extra days to "return" to one's ancestral village. Her dream, however, was to become a part of the Wong family that had remained in China.

She wrote to her grandfather's nephew, Wong Yuk Liang, at Bak Sa Village, explaining her desire not only to learn about the life of the people but also to have a chance to live it. Yuk Liang, a middle-school teacher who had taught himself English, responded, "Glad to know you are my relationship and come back to sight seeing and learning some life of peasants in our motherland." He concluded with a warm invitation.

While most returning overseas Chinese travel to their ancestral villages by hired car, Pamela elected to take the bus from Canton to Toising, the county capital, where Yuk Liang would meet her. From the moment she squeezed through the crowds onto the bus and climbed over the luggage blocking the aisle, nothing went right. Because of bad weather, they had to wait five hours for a seven-minute ferry crossing. As the journey stretched to twelve hours, cigarette smoke choked the air. She fretted over what she would do if Yuk Liang wasn't at the station, and how they would find each other even if he was, for neither knew what the other looked like.

By the time the bus made a dinner and refueling stop, Pamela wanted to scream with impatience and worry. When it finally pulled into the station at ten that evening, she was as embarrassed as she was relieved when the bus driver, taking her under his wing, shouted into the crowd, "Who is looking for Wong Mei Qin? Who is looking for Wong Mei Qin?"

Yuk Liang stepped forward; they clasped hands and greeted each other, he in broken English, she in broken Chinese. Having missed the last bus to the village, they had to spend the night in a local hotel. Pamela's bed on the women's floor was one of four in the room. The communal toilet was broken, the "bathtub" simply a room with a tap, bare floor, and barred, curtainless window. But it cost only fifty cents.

The next day Yuk Liang gave her a tour of Toising before they boarded the bus for Bak Sa. Yuk Liang's sons were waiting for them at the bus stop in a pouring rain. Securing Pamela's suitcase and guitar onto the bicycles, they headed home with Pamela perched precariously on the back, clinging to the cyclist with one arm and hanging onto an umbrella with the other. The family's warm welcome, however, made her feel like a close relative. She called Yuk Liang, Uncle; his wife, Auntie; and their children, all adults, brothers and sisters.

Like many other Chinese, Pamela's relatives believed that everyone in America is rich; the morning after her arrival, Yuk Liang and his wife told her they wanted $2,500 to build a new house. Pamela knew that for almost a century, the people in Toishan had depended on remittances sent home from relatives overseas and that when the Communist victory in 1949 severed communication between the families in Toishan and America, the people had suffered terribly. But since the seventies, the flow of remittances had been restored. In Toising, the Children's Palace, the science school, and the hospital that she had seen the day before had all been built with contributions from overseas Chinese. Nevertheless, her uncle and aunt's request for money caught Pamela unaware, and when they persisted despite her protestations, she felt badgered.

It took an entire day for her to convince them she could not give them the money, longer to persuade them to let her help in the daily chores. Gradually she became a part of the family and her days settled into the routine of daily village life. "Most mornings, I 'took tea' [breakfasted] with Uncle and my brothers at the Sin Sin Cha Lou, New Tea House. Besides myself, only one other woman ate there regularly. And on the days that I didn't join Uncle for breakfast, I enjoyed a simple meal of rice gruel at home with Auntie."

The youngest daughter, Xiao Heng, became Pamela's confidante and teacher. After breakfast, they would go to the fields and tend to the vegetables, harvesting the ones that were ready or pulling weeds. "When it was too hot in the fields for me, I stayed at the house with Auntie or watched Xiao Heng's two boys, ages four and twenty months, while Auntie played *mah-jong* with the neighbors. The family was very patient with my ignorance of rural customs, and they encouraged me to try common tasks such as keeping the cooking fire lit and planting rice."

She wrote in her diary, "This is what I've been looking for. Being thrust into the daily culture, having to learn the language, customs, and everyday way of life." Of these three, language was the most difficult.

Pamela spoke halting basic Mandarin, but the dialect spoken in the village was Toishanese. In over a century of travel between Toishan and America, many English

Two traditions still widely observed among Chinese in America are the celebration of the Lunar New Year and the visiting and cleaning of graves at Ching Ming, the annual festival that occurs around Easter. Here, in a California suburb, children play at lion dancing during the Lunar New Year. (Courtesy Him Mark Lai)

words—such as *welcome, steak, tie, pass, film, outside*—had been incorporated into the local language, and there were combinations of English and Chinese words—such as *walk lo* (road), *da* (play) *ball, loh* (old) *man*—interspersed in their speech as well. The family's youngest son had studied English in school, and Yuk Liang had taught himself English and also spoke Mandarin—all of which allowed for communication at a functional level. But any expression of thoughts and feelings was impossible.

Nevertheless, she said, "Every day taught me something different about China and her people, and I, in turn, taught the family a little of my world in the United States."

During her three-month stay, Pamela sometimes borrowed a bicycle and went exploring on her own. Riding along the dirt roads, she thought of her ancestors for whom this was home. Her great-great-grandparents had left over a hundred years before. But the sons from each generation had returned to Bak Sa for a wife, at first because there were so few Chinese women in America to choose from, and then because they wanted old-fashioned wives.

Her grandfather, Stacy, had been the last son to go back. The year was 1931, and arranged marriages were still common, though not necessarily "blind." The matchmakers had given him an opportunity to indicate his preference from a selection of suitable candidates:

At Ching Ming, members of the same family clan honor their ancestors in Woon Ben Village, China, and in Washington, D.C. (Courtesy Betty Woon Jung)

Some Chinese Americans who have lived and worked in China have discovered that the homeland they were looking for is, in fact, America. As one woman put it, "Before, I always said I was Chinese. After all, my family always spoke Chinese and ate Chinese food. I went there and I was more American than I realized. Now, if somebody were to ask me, I'd say I'm American." And while Pamela (standing directly behind Auntie, who is seated) considers her three months in Bak Sa a return to her roots, she acknowledged, "I'm an American. I grew up in America, speak English, attended American schools, eat American food. The Chinese in me comes from inside. From my thirst to discover that part of me that is hidden behind generations in the United States." (Courtesy Pamela Wong)

twenty-four young women were told, under various pretexts, to go look for fabric at a certain store.

One by one Stacy inspected the women as they browsed over bolts of fabric. None of them appealed to him, and he was about to leave when he noticed Jin Hao. A beautiful girl of seventeen with a long, thick braid, she had been persuaded to shop in Bak Sa, as the store offered a better selection of fabrics. Only when she glanced up from the piece of material she was examining did she realize that she was being scrutinized.

"It was love at first sight," she told Pamela years later.

The match was made and the couple settled in Portland. Their own sons chose brides in America. Pamela was the first Wong to go back in half a century.

During her brief tour of Toising, she had seen the influence of returning emigrants in the architecture, the pool halls, the coffee shop that served barbecued pork sandwiches, pancakes, waffles, and French toast with syrup. The poverty that had driven her ancestors overseas was also evident in the thrift that she saw everywhere. "The peelings from sugarcane are dried and then burned for fuel for cooking. Leftover food is served until it is no longer left over. Used by the body for energy, it is then given back to fertilize the land. Wine, soda, and soy sauce bottles are all used over and over again. And every possible square foot of land is used efficiently and with purpose."

While some people might have been appalled by these conditions, Pamela felt it a privilege to take part in the daily life of a Chinese peasant family. "To think that this family is related to mine was—and still is—incredible," she says.

Currently working as a secretary for a China trade consulting firm, Pamela hopes some day to be a consultant herself. She is also anxious to learn more about her heritage. "My dream is to make it back to Bak Sa in the near future to spend a year with my family there," she said. "To get back to my roots in the land. To *really* get to know the kind of life my ancestors lived."

Ho Yuet Fung
(Courtesy Ho Yuet Fung)

Ho Yuet Fung,
Immigrant

Ho Yuet Fung, a Hong Kong television scriptwriter, was all set to accompany her boyfriend, an artist, to Paris for a year when a former classmate from the Chinese University told her about a graduate scholarship in broadcast journalism at the University of Missouri. "I had never thought of going to America, but I was very practical. The scholarship meant I could stay abroad for two years instead of one, so I applied."

After her acceptance, she wrote acquaintances at the university to arrange for housing. "They said I could room with them but to bring lots of towels because they were very expensive and a cleaver because that kind of knife was unavailable."

Armed with both, Yuet Fung arrived in Columbia, Missouri, in the wake of a storm that had left over a foot of snow. Her initial impressions of America were of the cold, the scarcity of people on the streets, and their reluctance to walk even short distances of a block or two. She also soon discovered that despite the friendliness of students and professors, she could not fit into the program's training process.

One of the criteria for the scholarship was that the applicant be an individual who had worked in the communications field for several years. Though only in her mid-twenties, Yuet Fung had worked as a newspaper reporter and written treatments, documentaries, and dramatic scripts for television. But the culture of Missouri in the 1970s was so alien to her that she could not grasp the issues sufficiently to write anything with depth. Even a simple assignment—creating an advertisement for a pizza—was difficult: What *was* a pizza? Nor did her limited schoolgirl English allow her to talk in front of a camera. Training sessions in English pronunciation only made her so self-conscious that she hesitated to speak at all.

If Yuet Fung had gone to Missouri as a traditional student, she would have been devastated. But she had left Hong Kong looking for adventure. "I wrote well about the young and the old, but I couldn't resolve women's issues, and the middle-aged characters I created were stereotypic. I felt I needed more experience with life itself."

The only people with whom she could communicate comfortably were overseas Chinese students, so she spent much of her time with them in late-night discussions. "What is China?" they asked themselves. "What

are we doing here?" Some students were simply looking for ways to become permanent residents. Most believed they would take back what they learned in America to improve their homeland. But as Yuet Fung listened to them talk, she realized that their futures and their choices were often limited by factors outside their control.

Many of those from Hong Kong would be overqualified for the jobs available to Chinese in the British Colony. If their politics allowed them to consider living and working in China as an alternative, they had more of a future—but these students were often better activists than scholars. Those from Taiwan seemed the least free, for any deviation from the Kuomintang party line, however innocent, meant stigmatization as pro-China and the risk of being blacklisted on their return home.

Finding Missouri confining, the students would sometimes drive to Chicago. These brief trips were not enough for Yuet Fung, who left to join her boyfriend in Paris. "The artists were all struggling, and people without money there are treated like outcasts. Chinese students lived in garrets. They always had to use the back door, and they couldn't break into French society without a French boyfriend or girlfriend," she recalled. "Suddenly Paris seemed dark and the United States like sunshine." After only a few weeks, she broke off with her boyfriend and returned to Chicago.

To gain fluency in English and learn more about American society, Yuet Fung worked as a waitress and then as a researcher. And she pondered her future. Though her main interest was in the creative aspects of film, she was also intrigued by new technology. In Hong Kong, technicians were very possessive of their knowledge, and she decided to focus on acquiring technical skills so she could communicate better with them when she returned.

"I never made a conscious decision not to go back to Hong Kong," she explained. "In fact, what kept me going during my first years in America was the thought that this was temporary." But after enrolling in the film program at Columbia University in New York, Yuet Fung met, then married, Boston-born filmmaker Stephen Ning.

She is still ambivalent about being an immigrant, however. "People here are not as tied to conventions as they are in Hong Kong. You can be independent and

Prior to leaving China for graduate school at the University of California at Los Angeles, Yu Renqiu (first from left) had very vague ideas about America. "Even though I had some awareness from reading American literature and magazines, I thought Americans were selfish people dominated by a desire for money and casual sex, that American kids were noisy, crazy about rock and roll and never studied," he recalled. Nor are Americans' perceptions of Chinese any more accurate. "They think Chinese are quiet, traditional, hardworking, and passive. Actually we are open-minded and aggressive." (Courtesy Yu Renqiu)

After his initial adjustment, he felt that Americans and Chinese were basically human beings who responded and dealt with life in much the same way. Now he believes, "Our cultures are very different. This society is so diverse. There are so many different ethnic groups. I feel frustrated. How can I learn about them all?" Currently a doctoral candidate in United States history at New York University, Yu plans to take the new ideas and methodologies he has learned in America back to China. In particular, he wants to take back the concept that all students should be treated equally. In his experience, students in America are treated fairly by their professors. "But in China, whites are treated the best, then Chinese Americans, then those from Hong Kong, then visiting or returning Chinese. Chinese who have never left China are at the bottom. It's a continuation of the semifeudal, semi-colonial mentality. Every educated person criticizes it, but it takes time to change." He acknowledged that, like many returning students, he will probably feel frustrated in his efforts to contribute. "But I believe that if everyone makes a conscious effort at change, then change can take place, whether in China or America." He is seen here with his roommate at the University of California at Los Angeles, Bruce True (left), who helped him learn English. (Courtesy Yu Renqiu)

Chinese immigrants in the late 1940s and early 1950s were a mix of political refugees—students, officials, and supporters of the Nationalist government in Taiwan—and war brides. Many of the political refugees, mainly wealthy non-Cantonese speakers from northern and eastern China, dismissed Chinese Americans, most of them southern Chinese, as "hillbillies." And though the war brides were usually from the same regions as their Chinese American husbands, they were not always compatible—frequently because the women found the reality of life in America far different from their fantasies of Gold Mountain. (Courtesy Oregon Historical Society)

Ho Yuet Fung met Stephen Ning while he was working as a cinematographer for her class project at Columbia University. Later she worked with him as assistant director, translator, and Chinese dialogue coach on his film Freckled Rice, *a semiautobiographical film that explores the cultural and linguistic conflicts experienced by two boys in Boston's Chinatown (above). A subtle combination of Chinese and English dialogue and nonverbal scenes,* Freckled Rice *vividly depicts what it means to live on the fringe. It has been featured at film festivals around the world and shown on national television, and has won numerous awards. (Courtesy Stephen Ning)*

Yuet Fung and Stephen agree that theirs is an intercultural marriage. "But we share the same basic principles and beliefs," Stephen said. When he visited his ancestral village in Toishan, Stephen was struck by the similarities between his father (above), who had left for America at nineteen, and his uncle (left), who had stayed behind. Both have suffered, his uncle as a member of an overseas Chinese family during China's Cultural Revolution, his father as a marginal man in America. Though they married and raised children under diametrically opposed political systems, they have passed down the same basic values and ideals to their children.
Now Stephen and Yuet Fung are combining their skills and talents on a new project, From Toishan to Cambridge, *in which they document and compare these two men and their families. (Courtesy Stephen Ning)*

The November 11, 1899, issue of Frank Leslie's Weekly noted, "Strip off {Chinatown's} profusion of ornament, and underneath there is nothing but the grim, black-halled, foul-aired, many-celled tenement houses." The same commentary applies today. Besides substandard, overcrowded housing, some of the many problems that plague Chinatown residents are unemployment and underemployment; high infant mortality, tuberculosis and death rates; lack of recreational facilities; and inadequate police protection and other resources. (Courtesy Robert Glick/New York Chinatown History Project)

Racial tension and brawls are a part of school life for many immigrant children. According to Bruce Kelley, project director for California Tomorrow, a nonprofit organization that works to promote harmony among the state's racial and ethnic groups, "Every single Asian immigrant we have interviewed gave accounts of being punched, made fun of, harassed, mimicked, or robbed by fellow students." Chinese immigrant parents often unwittingly increase the burden on their children by blaming them for the attacks, believing that if their children would simply bai hoi, stand aside, such incidents would not occur. (Courtesy Robert Glick/New York Chinatown History Project)

strive for what you want to do. But I still dream of going back because my English is not good enough for me to write well. And there's so much I still don't understand. The grant and nonprofit systems for independent filmmakers like myself are so complicated it's difficult to find out how to break in. In Hong Kong, where I was already in the system, I would be able to move much faster. Here I'm still looking for the way, for what to do with film."

Nevertheless, Yuet Fung realizes she has been far more fortunate than the majority of immigrants. Older professionals are often forced by their language limitations into menial occupations. Having given up family, friends, and well-paid jobs for their children's future, their demands for their children's success often border on the fanatical. Language can also be a barrier for young people, especially teenagers. Students unable to learn English quickly enough to meet their parents' unrealistic expectations frequently feel like failures. Some become truant, easy targets for recruiters for youth gangs. The elderly face other problems, as described by one woman: "Here we are like the disabled. We're deaf because we cannot understand the language.

We're dumb because we cannot speak it. We're blind because we cannot read it. And we're lame because we cannot find our way around."

New York's Chinatown, like Chinatowns in other metropolitan areas, is a ghetto. But Yuet Fung and her husband, Stephen, have chosen to live there. Both grew up in working-class neighborhoods. At the university in Hong Kong, Yuet Fung had majored in journalism because she thought "being a reporter is like being a king without a crown. You can create changes and bring about social justice." The reality was that the status of a Chinese-language newspaper reporter was very low, and the salary so poor that when she was offered the opportunity to train as a scriptwriter for television, she seized it. Nevertheless, her commitment to working people has never wavered, and all her writing, in Hong Kong and America, has dealt with social issues.

Now in New York, Yuet Fung has been documenting the struggle of Chinese restaurant workers to unionize. According to census figures (which do not reflect illegal aliens), one of every six Chinese in America works in the restaurant industry. Kitchen workers put

The United States government provided airfare to San Francisco and thirteen dollars, seven of which went for cab fare to Chinatown. "Luckily the manager of a residential hotel let us stay even though we had no money." Chaw, already fifty-seven years old, got a job the next day as a deliveryman for an import/export firm, and his wife, who had not worked in Cuba, became one of Chinatown's many "sewing women." Chaw recalled, "It was hard to start all over again. We lived in the hotel for four years, sharing a communal kitchen. And, after learning Spanish, my parents now had to learn English. But hardest of all was adjusting to the Chinese here. In Cuba, Chinese were less rigid, more open minded, and friendly—warmer, like the Latins. The Chinese here seem cold and reserved. Chinese Americans don't accept us and overseas Chinese look down on us because Cuba is a poor country." (Courtesy Gladys Chaw)

In the 1970s, political circumstances forced Chinese, many of whom had never lived in China, to emigrate from Cuba, Burma, and Indochina. Some of them, like Fernando Chaw, were making a second emigration. Chaw, whose first emigration was from China to Cuba in the 1920s, had finally saved enough to open a small grocery just before Castro came into power. Reluctant to give up the fruits of a lifetime's labor, he delayed leaving Cuba until 1962, when his three daughters became threatened by a new directive ordering girls to work in the sugar fields.

Since his eldest daughter had been born in San Francisco while he and his wife were in transit to Cuba, the family was able to seek refuge in America. They were permitted to take almost nothing out of Cuba. "We were each allowed three outfits, including the one we were wearing, one sweater, one towel, and one wedding ring if it was plain," his daughter, Gladys, remembered. "But our towels were confiscated at the airport."

In addition to researching the past, the New York Chinatown History Project records contemporary life in the community. Said director Charlie Lai, "History is always in the making. It's not the army generals who make history. It is the people who establish a community and make it live from day to day, from year to year, and from decade to decade." (Courtesy Robert Glick/New York Chinatown History Project)

in ten- to twelve-hour days, seven days a week for less than $400 a month and no benefits. Dining room workers—except where tips are turned in to the management—make slightly more despite a base pay of about $200 a month. Usually there is no sick leave or other benefits. When workers are ill, they are responsible for locating and paying substitutes to work in their place. Those who protest are told, "You don't have to work here." Unable to speak English, they really have no choice. In Manhattan, it was not until June 1978 that a Chinese restaurant finally unionized.

Only a handful of restaurants have since followed suit. Part of the appeal of Chinese food for the public is its inexpensiveness, and frequently the restaurant owners' profit margins are too slender to allow for union wages. With newer and bigger restaurants constantly opening, the competition is fierce, and many smaller establishments are being forced out of business. At the same time, the steady influx of new immigrants keeps competition for jobs fierce; conditions for illegals are particularly bad since their complaints are easily silenced with threats of deportation. Fighting for survival, owners and workers are trapped in an atmosphere of exploitation, mutual distrust, and powerlessness. In some cases, owners threatened with unionization sell out, owing workers back wages that are never paid. In

*Coin-operated laundries are replacing the old hand laundries, but all family members are still expected to pitch in and help with the work. Buck Wong, a laundry worker's son, said bitterly, "When it came to a decision of whether I should study for my test or help with the work, I always worked. I knew my father wanted me to get a good education. But at that moment he forgot all about it. I'd say that I wanted to go out to the library. He would say, 'Why do you have to go so much?' He would never let me out. I really hated the place."
(Courtesy Robert Glick/New York Chinatown History Project)*

Conditions at shirt presses are also harsh. "The heat is always ninety degrees or higher. We tie handkerchiefs around our foreheads, but the sweat still comes into the eyes and blinds you. Men get burned all the time from the steam and touching the machines." Pay is three cents a shirt, and it takes approximately three minutes to do one, though some pressers are faster. (Courtesy Paul Calhoun/New York Chinatown History Project)

*Not all immigrants are struggling. Leslie Tang owns and manages a portfolio of real estate estimated to be worth about $38 million. She is one of a number of rich professionals from Hong Kong and Taiwan, many of them educated at top universities in the United States. Instead of laboring in menial jobs, these immigrants develop office buildings, suburban shopping malls, and large housing developments. (Courtesy Gordon Stone/*San Francisco Examiner*)*

According to the June 30, 1986, New York Times, *the total number of immigrants—including illegals—currently entering the United States each year is .3 percent of the total population (as opposed to 1.5 percent at the historic peak). The Reverend Theodore M. Hesburgh, former member of the Select Commission on Immigration and Refugee Policy, has pointed out, "The genius of America is that we bring in genetic stock from all over the world. We need immigration." (Courtesy Paul Calhoun/ New York Chinatown History Project)*

other cases, employees are part owners, further complicating the issue.

While recording history in the making, Yuet Fung has also been researching the history of the Chinese in America at the New York Chinatown History Project. The founders of the project—Charles Lai, a community activist, and Jack Tchen, a social historian—acknowledged, "A history of Chinatown won't buy rice, and it won't provide heat in the winter." But they also insisted, "If younger generations do not understand the hardships and triumphs of their elders, then we will be a people without a past."

Yuet Fung agrees. Moreover, before her involvement with Chinese American history, she did not distinguish between Chinese Americans and Chinese. When she first met Stephen, she assumed they shared the same history and culture as well as race. Now she recognizes their myriad differences. "As a girl in Hong Kong, the discrimination I felt was generalized British exploitation, not specific. So I have a stronger sense of identity and more confidence than most Chinese Americans because I didn't have to confront racism until I came to America. By then I was an adult. Chinese Americans are also more angry and bitter because this is their country. But even though we are so different, I identify with them because they are fighting for the same issues I care about: rights, justice, and equality."

Exploring these issues in the context of Chinese American history, she made a film about the hand laundries, *Eight Pound Livelihood,* based on oral histories gathered under the auspices of the Chinatown History Project. As one interviewee said, "Laundries in the 1920s and 30s were like today's candy stores, one in every block." In letters home, the men—too proud to admit they washed dirty clothes—would refer to them as "clothing shops."

Sons who had lived in luxury in Hong Kong and China were shocked when they joined their fathers. "We got up at 5:00 AM and worked until 1:00 AM. Then we slept on a two-foot-wide wooden board laid on top of two milk boxes." Wives "lucky" enough to join their husbands labored alongside while raising families in back rooms. "I worked and carried my children until I had varicose veins. The veins became like balls and I wrapped them with cloth around my legs," one woman told her. Another woman added, "I didn't mind the work. I can't speak, but my hands and feet can do something. It's the loneliness I can't bear."

Yuet Fung, still uncomfortable writing in English, has also created a Cantonese radio drama, *Jin Chai: A Woman's Journey into Chinese America.* The journey of the heroine, Jin Chai, from Kwantung to New York in the 1930s, her passage from one culture to another, and her struggle to adjust to a new environment echo Yuet Fung's own journey. She has discovered, "Learning about the history of the Chinese in America has given me strength as a new immigrant, a feeling that I am not drifting, a sense of roots."

Some Major Legislation
Affecting Chinese in America

Special Taxes

Chinese began emigrating to California in large numbers during the Gold Rush. Mexicans and South Americans who preceded the Chinese had been driven out of the gold fields by a Foreign Miners' Tax, and in 1852, the California State Legislature tried to drive the Chinese out by re-enacting this law, charging Chinese miners a monthly tax of three dollars. This fee was increased to four dollars the following year. Nevertheless, enough Chinese remained so that from 1850 to 1870—when the law was voided by an amendment to the United States Constitution—half the state's income was derived from this source.

Special mining taxes were enacted in other states; then the taxes were extended from mining to other industries in which Chinese worked. Chinese fishermen in California, for example, had to pay a monthly license fee of four dollars; in Oregon's Jackson and Josephine counties, a monthly fee of fifty dollars was levied against Chinese engaged in any kind of trading.

Exclusion Laws

In 1868, the United States and China signed the Burlingame Treaty, which recognized the right of recip-rocal immigration, privileges, immunities, and exemptions between the two nations. Two years later, the California State Legislature passed an act denying Chinese women immigrants the right of entry unless they could prove to the Commissioner of Immigration that they were "of correct habits and good character." The 1875 Page Law and the California State Constitution adopted in 1879 added further restrictions to the immigration of Chinese laborers and women deemed to be prostitutes.

Then, in 1882, the United States Congress passed the Chinese Exclusion Act, suspending the immigration of Chinese laborers, both skilled and unskilled, for ten years. Teachers, students, merchants, and travelers were exempt from this prohibition, but no Chinese would be permitted naturalization. The Geary Act of May 5, 1892, extended the Exclusion Act for ten more years; on April 27, 1904, the exclusion of Chinese laborers from the United States and its island territories was extended indefinitely.

Laws were also passed to decrease the number of Chinese already in America. The Scott Act of October 1, 1888, prohibited the return of any Chinese laborers

During Exclusion, General John "Blackjack" Pershing helped more than 500 Chinese men gain entry to America through a special act of Congress. To him, it was a debt of honor. In 1916, he had led 10,000 troops into Mexico in pursuit of "Pancho" Villa, who had killed 17 Americans just north of the border. The United States Army's supply trucks suffered repeated machine failures in the deserts and mountains of Chihuahua. But Mexico's President, fearing for the stability of his government, denied the Americans permission to use the railroad. Mexican civilians refused to help.

What saved Pershing and his men were Chinese who hauled in needed goods on two-horse wagons and then, after the Mexican government forbade Chinese use of the public highways, smuggled in supplies on horses, mules, and on foot. By the time Pershing received orders to return to America, there were 527 Chinese attached to the expeditionary force, and Villa publicly vowed to kill every one.

Pershing, refusing to leave behind the men who had served him so loyally, secured special permission to take them with him. For the next five years, "Pershing's Chinese" were interned at Fort Sam Houston, Texas, while he and his friend William Tracy Page lobbied Congress on their behalf—at first for United States citizenship, and then, when that was denied, for permanent residence, which was finally granted.

During their internment, the men were not idle. They dug trenches and performed other labor for the military for twenty cents an hour. Through special "chop suey dinners," they raised substantial amounts of money for the American Red Cross, the local Christmas Empty Stocking Fund, and the French War Orphans Fund. After their release, they settled in San Antonio, where many of their descendants live today. (Courtesy Library of Congress)

As long as Chinese were denied the right to become naturalized citizens, they continued to be involved in China's politics while living in America. A few white Americans, including Homer Lea, also became involved. In 1903, Lea—reputed to be a master of modern warfare, even a military genius—established a network of schools across the country to train officers for a reformed Chinese army. Since no group of aliens is permitted to bear arms as a military organization in America, training had to be carried out under strict secrecy. For his drill sergeant in the first school in Los Angeles, Lea hired Ansel O'Banion, a former sergeant with three years of distinguished service as a scout in the Fourth Cavalry. O'Banion, in turn, enlisted his friends from the Fourth Cavalry to train companies in thirty other cities. The men they trained were almost exclusively Chinese already in America, men who worked in laundries, restaurants, and stores during the day. But there were also 250 sons of Chinese officials who were brought from China for training. (Courtesy Albert and Joshua Powers)

who had departed from the United States. At the time it was passed, over 20,000 Chinese laborers had temporarily left the United States for China with re-entry certificates. These permits were declared void.

Section Three of the Cable Act, passed on September 22, 1922, stipulated that any female citizen who married an alien ineligible for citizenship "shall cease to be a citizen of the United States. If at the termination of the marital status she is a citizen of the United States she shall retain her citizenship, regardless of her residence." This meant that any American woman who married a Chinese would lose her citizenship. Non-Chinese women would be able to apply for and regain their citizenship if they divorced or became widowed. But women of Chinese ancestry would never be able to regain their original legal status since Chinese were ineligible for citizenship.

Until 1924, wives of Chinese merchants and wives of American-born Chinese were allowed to enter the country for permanent residence, although wives of Chinese laborers were barred. After passage of the 1924 Immigration Act, *no* Chinese women were allowed to enter the United States for the purpose of permanent residence. In 1925, the Supreme Court ruled that merchants' wives were admissable. Five years later, an amendment to the Cable Act also permitted the entry of alien wives who had been married to United States citizens prior to 1924.

Alien Land Laws

The Alien Land Laws, passed in California in 1913 and 1921, were orginally aimed at Japanese but were amended in 1923 and 1927 to cover all Asians. Other states with Alien Land Laws were Arizona, Idaho, Oregon, Washington, and Montana. Until the laws were declared unconstitutional in 1947, Chinese, as aliens ineligible for citizenship, were denied the right to buy or own land.

Anti-miscegenation Laws

States forbidding marriages between whites and people of color, including Chinese, were Arizona, California, Georgia, Idaho, Louisiana, Mississippi, Missouri, Nebraska, Nevada, South Dakota, Utah, Virginia, and Wyoming. At least one official interpreted the law to include anyone who was part Caucasian, thus preventing a Chinese man in Utah from marrying a black woman that the official considered mulatto. In some states these laws were not struck down until the United States Supreme Court decision in 1967.

Born in Portland, Oregon, Clara Lee (wearing hat) was an American citizen by birth. As soon as California women won suffrage in 1911, she and her friend Emma Leung registered to vote. Standing behind the women are their husbands. (Courtesy Dr. Lester Lee)

Other Laws

Along with blacks and Native Americans, Chinese were prohibited in some states from testifying for or against whites, and their children were forced to attend segregated schools. Additional laws were targeted specifically at the Chinese. For example, in San Francisco, the Sidewalk Ordinance of 1870 prohibited people who used poles to carry merchandise from walking on the sidewalk. The Chinese fought all these laws in the courts and, one by one, they were declared unconstitutional.

Repeal

Exclusion was repealed on December 18, 1943. Though only 105 Chinese immigrants were allowed each year (compared to 60,000 for England), Chinese could now become naturalized citizens. This miniscule quota was extended through passage of specific legislation, such as the War Brides Act of 1945, which allowed the wives of American servicemen to enter the United States. The Displaced Persons Act (1948), the Refugee Relief Act (1953), and a special Presidential Directive (1962) also permitted the immigration of close to 25,000 Chinese outside the quota. But it wasn't until the Immigration Act of October 3, 1965 (effective July 1, 1968), that the national-origin quota system was abolished.

Signed by President Lyndon B. Johnson at the foot of the Statue of Liberty, this historic act provided a quota

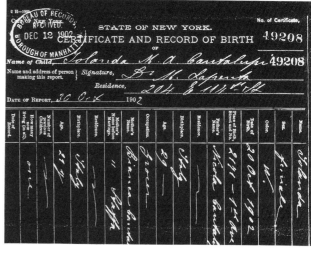

Among the many restrictive laws passed during Exclusion was the 1922 Cable Act, under which any woman who married an "alien ineligible for citizenship" would lose her United States citizenship. New York-born Yolanda Cantalupi was one of the women who lost her citizenship as a result of this law. While a student at Barnard, she had met and fallen in love with Francis Fay, a graduate of Columbia University. Since Fay was born in Canton, China, he was ineligible for citizenship though he had lived in America since he was fourteen. When Cantalupi married him on July 6, 1925, she immediately lost her own citizenship, though she did not realize it until she attempted to vote and was not permitted to do so. The law was never repealed; it was amended, so that she—and other women in her situation (most of them Chinese Americans)—had to go through naturalization in order to get back the citizenship that was theirs by right of birth. (Courtesy Rosemarie Fay Loomis)

of up to 20,000 per year for each independent country outside of the Western Hemisphere. This quota was attributed to the alien's country of birth, not nationality or race. China and Taiwan shared a quota for 20,000. Persons born in Hong Kong were charged to Great Britain's quota; the number permitted could not exceed one percent of the total visas issued to Great Britain in one year. Thus, the average waiting period for a visa for would-be immigrants from Hong Kong was eight years.

Recent Legislation

After the normalization of United States—China relations in 1979, China was allocated a quota of 20,000. In 1982, the Reagan administration awarded Taiwan a quota of 20,000. Under the new Immigration Act passed in 1986, the quota for persons born in Hong Kong was expanded to 5,000.

The 1986 Immigration Act also permits the legalization of aliens who have been living illegally in the United States before January 1, 1982, but the provisions are so complicated and the wording so poor that it seems to be generating more confusion and pain than relief. And the stipulations for the fining and even jailing of employers who hire undocumented aliens create a climate of fear that affects all aliens.

In November 1986, California voters passed an "English-Only" proposition, making English the official language of the state. Proponents are now trying to push a federal "English-Only" constitutional amendment through Congress. They are also lobbying the Federal Communications Commission to curtail licensing renewals for television and radio stations broadcasting in Chinese, Spanish, or any language other than English.

In a 1979 interview, Henry Der—Executive Director of Chinese for Affirmative Action in San Francisco—said, "Chinese Americans are still disenfranchised. There's inadequate police protection and other services because we lack political influence. One does not see many Chinese Americans in leadership roles in government." A March 1986 study of San Francisco's government by Chinese for Affirmative Action found little had changed. There were still few Asian faces in positions of decisive power. And of forty-two major city departments, only one, the Community College District Board, was headed by a Chinese American.

The situation is the same, or worse, in other cities. Virginia Kee, who helped establish the New York Chinatown Planning Council in 1964, warned, "Even though you have an education and security, if you don't have political power, you don't have anything." (Courtesy Chinese Culture Foundation Collection, Asian American Studies Library, University of California at Berkeley)

Selected Bibliography

Yung Wing and the Chinese Educational Mission

Chinese Educational Mission. Eugene Clarence Gardener Papers. Yale University Archives.

Chinese Educational Mission. Social scrapbooks assembled by Phyllis Kihn. Connecticut Historical Society, Hartford.

Chinese Educational Mission. The Thomas Edward La Fargue Papers. Washington State University Archives, Pullman.

Chinn, Thomas W. "Backdrop for Research." *Chinese Historical Society of America Bulletin*, January 1966.

Kao, Timothy K. "An American Sojourn: Young Chinese Students in the United States 1872–1881." *Connecticut Historical Society Bulletin*, July 1981.

Ko Kun Hua. Papers Relating to Instruction in Chinese 1877–1882. Harvard University Archives.

La Fargue, Thomas E. *China's First Hundred.* Pullman: The State College of Washington Press, 1942.

Lee, Yan Phou. *When I Was a Boy in China.* Boston: D. Lothrop Co., 1887.

Leung, Edwin Pak-wah. "The Education of Early Chinese Students in America." *The Chinese American Experience: Papers from the Second National Conference on Chinese American Studies.* San Francisco, 1980.

Liang, Che Chiang. Correspondence of Liang Tun-yen, Liang Che Chiang, Martin Welles, and Roger Welles. Connecticut Historical Society, Hartford.

Williams, Helen G. "International Living—An Old Experiment." *New England Galaxy*, Winter 1966.

Yung, Wing. Diary of Yung Wing (1902). Connecticut State Library Archives, Hartford.

Yung, Wing. *My Life in China and America.* New York: Henry Holt & Co., 1909.

Yung, Wing. Papers. Yale University Archives.

Mary Bong, Frontierswoman

DeArmond, Robert N. Letters to author. August 20, 1986 and September 22, 1986.

Fessler, Loren W., Ed. *Chinese in America: Stereotyped Past, Changing Present.* New York: Vantage Press, 1983.

Hatch, Heather, and Fong, Lawrence. "The Chinese Experience." *Scottsdale Progress*, September 8, 1979.

Hirata, Lucie Cheng. "Chinese Immigrant Women in Nineteenth-Century California." In *Women of America*, edited by C. R. Berkin and M. B. Norton. Boston: Houghton Mifflin Co., 1979.

Hirata, Lucie Cheng. "Free, Endentured, Enslaved: Chinese Prostitutes in Nineteenth Century America." *Signs*, Autumn 1979.

Huang, Yaofu. Letter to Tsai Nuliang. October 1, 1984.

Kwock, Marilyn. Letter to author. August 4, 1986.

McCunn, Ruthanne Lum. *Thousand Pieces of Gold.* San Francisco: Design Enterprises of San Francisco, 1981.

Pearson, Grant H. "My Home, My Country." *Alaska Sportsman*, May 1950.

Tang, Vincente. "Chinese Women Immigrants and the Two-Edged Sword of Habeas Corpus." *The Chinese American Experience: Papers from the Second National Conference on Chinese American Studies.* San Francisco, 1980.

Topley, Marjorie. "Marriage Resistance in Rural Kwangtung." In *Women in Chinese Society*, edited by Marjorie Wolf and Roxanne Witke. Stanford: Stanford University Press, 1975.

(Unknown.) "Local News." *Sitka Alaskan*, October 12, 1895.

Wheeler, Denice. *The Feminine Frontier: Wyoming Women 1850–1900.* Evanston, Wyoming: self-published, 1987.

Lue Gim Gong, Horticulturist

Bitters, Dr. William. Letter to author. May 29, 1987.

Burlingames. Genealogy. Rhode Island Historical Society, Providence.

Coogan, Tim. *The Forging of a Small New England Mill Town: North and South Adams, Massachusetts, 1780–1880.* Ph.D. dissertation, New York University, 1988.

Dreggors, Bill. Interview with author. DeLand, Florida, May 1986.

Hagstrom, Ruth. Interview with author. Pierson, Florida, May 1986.

Hagstrom, Ruth. Letters to author. 1986 and 1987.

Lew, Duk Gwong. Interview with author. Toishan, China, December 1985.

Lew, Duk Sum. Interview with author. Toishan, China, December 1985.

Lew, Yao Huan. Interviews with author. San Francisco, California, September 1985 and January 1986.

Lue, Gim Gong. Genealogy. Lew Duk Sum, Toishan, China.

Lue, Gim Gong. Papers. Dr. Chih Meng, White Plains, New York.

Lue, Gim Gong. Papers. Helena Friese, Jacksonville, Florida.

Lue, Gim Gong. Papers. Him Mark Lai, San Francisco, California.

Lue, Gim Gong. Papers. North Adams Public Library, North Adams, Massachusetts.

Lue, Gim Gong. Papers. Stetson University Archives, DeLand, Florida.

Reynolds, George Lee. Interview with Christine Richardson. Rockaway, Oregon, February 1978.

Van Cleef, Alice. Interview with author. DeLand, Florida, May 1986.

Notes

Lue Gim Gong's year of birth is variously recorded as 1858 and 1860 and cannot be confirmed.

Neither the Lue Gim Gong orange nor Gim Gong grapefruit is now considered a separate variety. Nevertheless, according to Dr. William Bitters, Professor of Horticulture, Emeritus, University of California at Riverside: "Although {Lue Gim Gong} did not obtain citrus hybrids in his hybridization attempts, he did recognize that the trees he selected from the seedlings were better than anything previously associated with those budlines. The trees were healthy, free of disease, vigorous, and productive. The fact that the industry readily accepted Lue's trees—in fact almost fought for them—illustrates that his nucellar contributions were great. . . . His efforts contributed greatly to the citrus industry of Florida and the acceptance of nucellars by the citrus industry of the world."

Mary and Joseph Tape and Their Fight for Education

Low, Victor. *The Unimpressible Race: A Century of Educational Struggle by the Chinese in San Francisco*. San Francisco: East/West Publishing Co., 1982.

Tang, Loretta and Theodore. Interview with author. Fairfield, California, October 1986.

Tape, Mary. Papers. Chinese Women of America Research Project, Chinese Culture Foundation of San Francisco.

(Unknown.) "Our Chinese Edison." *San Francisco Daily Examiner*, August 4, 1889.

(Unknown.) "What a Chinese Girl Did." *San Francisco Morning Call*, August 4, 1889.

Chin Gee-hee, Railroad Baron

Anderson, Fay. "Chinese Riot and Massacre of September 2, 1885." Unpublished manuscript. Wyoming State Archives.

Chen, Wenjun. Interview with author. Toishan, China, December 1985.

Cheng, Lucie, and Liu, Yuzun with Zheng, Dehua. "Chinese Emigration, the Sunning Railroad and the Development of Toisan." *Amerasia Journal*, Spring/Summer 1982.

Chin, Art. *A History of the Chinese in Washington, 1857–1977*. Seattle, 1977.

Chin, Doug and Art. *Uphill, The Settlement and Diffusion of the Chinese in Seattle*. Seattle: Shorey Publications, 1973.

Chin, Gee-hee. Letters to Thomas Burke, 1909–1924. Him Mark Lai, San Francisco.

Griego, Andrew. "Rebuilding the California Southern Railroad: The Personal Account of a Chinese Labor Contractor, 1884." *Journal of San Diego History*, Fall 1979.

Guilbert, David C. "Tacoma's Expulsion of the Chinese." *Tacoma News Tribune*, September 18, 1983.

Hildebrand, Lorraine Barker. *Straw Hats, Sandals and Steel: The Chinese in Washington State*. Tacoma: Washington State American Revolution Bicentennial Commission, 1977.

Holubek, Linda Sue. "A Vital Hyphen: A Study of the Life and Influence of Helen Wong Jean (1903–   )." Paper, Blackburn College, Illinois, 1979.

Hoy, William. "Ah Louis." *Chinese Historical Society of America Bulletin*, January 1976.

Jean, Helen Wong. Letters to author, 1986 and 1987.

Mumann, John M. "War in the Mines." *In Wyoming*, Summer 1976.

Olsen, Doris. "U.S. History Written Around Ah Louis Family." *Vancouver Chinatown News*, March 3, 1977.

(Unknown.) "Ah Louis." *Los Angeles Chinatown 1980 Souvenir Book*.

(Unknown.) "Chin Gee Hee, Noted Seattle Chinese, Dead." *Seattle Times*, July 1, 1929.

(Unknown.) "Chinamen Embark for Native Land." *Rock Springs Rocket*, November 13, 1925.

(Unknown.) "Six Widows May Keep Chin Riches from Seattle Girl." *Seattle Times*, July 1, 1929.

(Unknown.) "Three Generations of Chinese Family Which Figures

in Queer Story of Wealth and Tradition." *Seattle Post Intelligencer*, September 23, 1917.

Wickersham, James. Letter to Herbert Hunt, April 21, 1916. Washington State Historical Society, Tacoma.

Note

Ah Louis's name was Wong On until his employer in San Luis Obispo told him, "All Chinese are either Wong or Charlie—Louis is more distinctive." So he took the name Ah Louis for himself and his store, and Louis is the surname that most of his descendants use.

Ing Hay, Healer, and Lung On, Entrepreneur

Barlow, Jeffrey, and Richardson, Christine. *China Doctor of John Day*. Portland: Binford & Mort, 1979.

Chen, Chia-lin. "A Gold Dream in the Blue Mountains, A Study of the Chinese Immigrants in the John Day Area, Oregon, 1870–1910." Master's thesis, Portland State University, 1972.

Davis, Lillian Peake. "Letter to the Editor." *Oregon Journal*, September 8, 1975.

Elsensohn, Sister M. Alfreda. *Idaho Chinese Lore*. Cottonwood: Idaho Corporation of Benedictine Sisters, 1979.

Mooney, Ted. "John Day's Chinese Papers Translated with New View of Area History as Aim." *Oregon Journal*, July 24, 1972.

Tang, Loretta and Theodore. Interview with author. Fairfield, California, October 1986.

Note

The formal names carved into the gravestones for Ing Hay and Lung On are Ng Yu Nim and Leung Kwong Wing. But the names they went by in John Day, Oregon, are Ing ("Doc") Hay and Lung "Leon" On, so those are the names that have been used here.

Wong Sing, Merchant Prince

Brown, Mike. "Wong Sing." *Vernal Express*, January 25, 1979.

Chen, Chong. Notes on back of photograph of Chen Chong and wife. Washington State Historical Society, Tacoma.

Daughters of Utah Pioneers. *Our Pioneer Heritage, The Early Chinese of Western United States*. Salt Lake City, 1967.

Lee, Cherylene. Interview with author. San Francisco, California, April 1987.

Morrill, A. Reed. "A Historical Study of Ashley Valley and its Environs." Master's thesis. Brigham Young University, 1937.

Papanikolas, Helen, ed. *The Peoples of Utah*. Salt Lake City: Utah State Historical Society, 1976.

Phillips, Helen Seeley. "Chinese Friend of the Red Man." *Frontier Times*, April/May 1968.

(Unknown.) "Wong Sing Dies in Truck Crash Monday." *Vernal Express*, March 22, 1934.

Wey, Nancy. "Fiddletown's Chinese Past." *San Francisco Sunday Examiner and Chronicle*, July 29, 1979.

Wong Sing. File Folder No. 166. Uintah County Library Regional Room, Vernal, Utah.

Li Khai Fai and Kong Tai Heong, Physicians and Community Leaders

Ai, Chung Kun. *My Seventy-Nine Years in Hawaii*. Hong Kong, 1960.

Bergin, Mrs. W. C. "Bubonic Plague in Hawaii, 1899–1900." *Paradise of the Pacific*, March 1945.

Char, Tin-Yuke, ed. *The Sandalwood Mountains: Readings and Stories of the Early Chinese in Hawaii.* Honolulu: The University Press of Hawaii, 1975.

Davey, Frank. "Through Plague and Fire in Honolulu, Hawaiian Islands." Unpublished manuscript. The Bishop Museum, Honolulu, Hawaii.

Glick, Clarence E. *Sojourners and Settlers: Chinese Migrants in Hawaii.* Honolulu: Hawaii Chinese History Center and the University Press of Hawaii, 1980.

Hawaii Board of Health. Minutes for October 21, 1896. Hawaii State Archives, Honolulu.

Iwamoto, Lana. "The Plague and Fire of 1899–1900." *Hawaii History Review,* July 1967.

Kong, Tai Heong. Day Books of Kong Tai Heong. Hawaii State Archives, Honolulu.

Li, Ling-Ai. *Life Is for a Long Time: A Chinese Hawaiian Memoir.* New York: Hastings House, 1972.

Li, Ling-Ai. "Together." *Paradise of the Pacific,* April 1956.

Soong, Irma Tam. "Li, Tai Heong Kong." In *Hawaii's Notable Women,* edited by Barbara Bennett. Honolulu: University of Hawaii Press, 1984.

U.S. Congress. House. "Payment of Judgments on Claims Growing Out of Suppression of Bubonic Plague in Hawaii." 57th Congress, 2nd Session. Report No. 3098.

Note

While all these sources agree that the first confirmed plague victim was a Chinese bookkeeper, Chong You, the attending physician is not always identified as Li Khai Fai. Iwamoto, disagreeing with the other sources listed above, identifies Dr. Sun Chin as the attending physician.

Arlee Hen and Black Chinese

Arizona Historical Society. *The Chinese Experience in Arizona and Northern Mexico.* Tucson, 1980.

Bernardi, Adria. "Heat in the Delta: Reactions to the Triangle." *Southern Exposure,* July/August 1984.

Black, Doris. "The Black Chinese." *Sepia,* January 1975.

Brown, Catherine, and Ganschow, Thomas. "The Augusta, Georgia, Chinese: 1865–1980." In *Georgia's East Asian Connection, 1733–1983,* edited by Jonathan Goldstein. West Georgia College Studies in the Social Sciences, 1983.

Chan, Berda Lum. Papers. Chinese Women of America Research Project, Chinese Culture Foundation of San Francisco.

Cohen, Lucy M. *Chinese in the Post–Civil War South: A People without a History.* Baton Rouge: Louisiana State University Press, 1984.

Hen, Arlee. Interview with Daisy Greene at Greenville, Mississippi, January 1977. Washington County Oral History Project, Mississippi Department of Archives and History, Jackson.

Hen, Arlee. Interview with Ho Yuet Fung at Greenville, Mississippi, May 1981. Mississippi Triangle Research Project, Third World Newsreel, New York City.

Hen, Arlee. Interview with Judy Yung at Greenville, Mississippi, December 1982. Chinese Women of America Research Project, Chinese Culture Foundation of San Francisco.

Lai, Violet L. *He Was a Ram.* Honolulu: Hawaii Chinese History Center and the University of Hawaii Press, 1985.

Lee, James. Letter to author. September 2, 1987.

Loewen, James W. *The Mississippi Chinese: Between Black and White.* Cambridge: Harvard University Press, 1971.

Quan, Robert Seto. *Lotus Among the Magnolias: The Mississippi Chinese.* Jackson: University Press of Mississippi, 1982.

Rummel, George Albert. *The Delta Chinese: An Exploratory Study in Assimilation.* Paper, University of Mississippi, 1964.

Solberg, S. E. "Sui Sin Far/Edith Eaton: First Chinese-American Fictionist." *Melus,* Spring 1981.

Sui Sin Far (Edith Eaton). "Leaves from the Mental Portfolio of an Eurasian." *Independent,* January 21, 1909.

Tajima, Renee. "Intersection in the Delta." *Southern Exposure,* July/August 1984.

(Unknown.) "A Chinese Colony." *New Orleans State Democrat,* November 12, 1899.

Works Progress Administration. *Louisiana: A Guide to the State.* 1941.

Chin Lung's Gold Mountain Promise

Chan, Sucheng. *This Bittersweet Soil: The Chinese in California Agriculture 1860–1910.* Berkeley: University of California Press, 1986.

Chan, Sucheng. "Chinese American Entrepreneur: The California Career of Chin Lung." In *Chinese America: History and Perspectives 1987,* edited by Him Mark Lai, Ruthanne Lum McCunn, and Judy Yung. San Francisco: Chinese Historical Society of America, 1987.

Chan, Sucheng. "The Chinese in California Agriculture, 1860–1900." *The Chinese American Experience: Papers from the Second National Conference on Chinese American Studies.* San Francisco, 1980.

Chew, Law Ying. Coaching Notes. Chew Law Ying, San Francisco, California.

Chew, Law Ying. Interviews with Judy Yung. San Francisco, California, September 1982 and January 1987.

Chin, Gway. Interview with Judy Yung. San Francisco, California, July 1979.

Chin, Wun Leung, and Chew, Jun Dai. Interview with Judy Yung. Namsan Village, China, December 1982.

Dunne, Geoffrey. "Atop the Golden Mountain: The Ow Legacy." *Good Times,* October 9, 1986.

Hing, Leah. Interview with Judy Yung. Portland, Oregon, April 1982.

Lei, Shu Quan. Interview with author. Toishan, China, December 1985.

Lew, So Ping. Interview with author. Toishan, China, December 1985.

Lew, Yao Huan. Interviews with author. San Francisco, California, September 1985 and January 1986.

Tang, Loretta and Theodore. Interview with author. Fairfield, California, October 1986.

Yung, Bick Heung. Interview with author. San Francisco, California, January 1987.

Yung, Hin Sen. Interview with Judy Yung. San Francisco, California, November 1986.

The Jung Family Album

Jung, Betty Woon. Interviews with author. San Francisco, California. Spring 1987.

Jung, Yuk Kwan. Interviews with Betty Woon Jung. Monterey, California, Spring 1987.

Tam, Fung Yung. Interviews with Betty Woon Jung. Monterey, California, Spring 1987.

The Lai Family, Reclaiming History

Chin, Art. Papers. Oregon Military Museum, Clackamas, Oregon.

Chinn, Thomas W., ed. *A History of the Chinese in California: A Syllabus*. San Francisco: Chinese Historical Society of America, 1969.

Choy, Philip. Interview with the author. San Francisco, California, June 1987.

Chung, L. A. "Sad Return of Chinese to Angel Island." *San Francisco Chronicle*, November 24, 1983.

Kaplan, Sam Hall. "Angel Island: Story of Chinese Immigration Lives On." *Los Angeles Times*, November 22, 1981.

Lai, Him Mark. "A Historical Survey of Organizations of the Left Among Chinese in America." *Bulletin of Concerned Asian Scholars*, Fall 1972.

Lai, Him Mark. "The History of the Bing Lai Family." Unpublished manuscript, Him Mark Lai, San Francisco, California.

Lai, Him Mark. *A History Reclaimed: An Annotated Bibliography of Chinese Language Materials on the Chinese in America*. Los Angeles: Asian American Studies Center, University of California, 1986.

Lai, Him Mark. Interviews with author. San Francisco, California, Spring 1987.

Lai, Him Mark; Lim, Genny; and Yung, Judy. *Island: Poetry and History of Chinese Immigration on Angel Island 1910–1940*. San Francisco: HOC DOI Project, 1980.

Nee, Victor G., and de Bary, Brett. *Longtime Californ': A Documentary Study of an American Chinatown*. Boston: Houghton Mifflin Co., 1974.

Richart, Philip (Oregon Military Museum). Letter to author, April 27, 1987.

(Unknown.) "The Search for a Golden Dream." *Asia Magazine*, May 20, 1984.

Yu, Connie Young. "Rediscovered Voices: Chinese Immigrants and Angel Island." *Amerasia Journal*, 1977.

Eleanor Wong Telemaque, American-Born and Foreign

Hom, Marlon K. *Songs of Gold Mountain: Cantonese Rhymes from San Francisco Chinatown*. Berkeley: University of California Press, 1987.

Hsu, Evelyn. "The Man Who'll Print Beijing Paper in San Francisco." *San Francisco Chronicle*, June 3, 1985.

Lam, Julie Shuk-yee. "The 'Chinese Digest,' 1935 to 1940." In *Chinese America: History and Perspectives 1987*, edited by Him Mark Lai, Ruthanne Lum McCunn, and Judy Yung. San Francisco: Chinese Historical Society of America, 1987.

Loomis, Rosemarie Fay. Interview with author. New Orleans, Louisiana, May 1986.

Moody, Fred. "Shawn Wong, Out from the Shadows." *Seattle Times/ Seattle Post Intelligencer*, January 19, 1986.

Mason, Sarah. "Family Structure and Acculturation in the Chinese Community in Minnesota." *The Chinese American Experience: Papers from the Second National Conference on Chinese American Studies*. San Francisco, 1980.

Nee, Victor G., and de Bary, Brett. *Longtime Californ': A Documentary Study of an American Chinatown*. Boston: Houghton Mifflin, 1974.

Telemaque, Eleanor Wong. Interviews with author. New York City, May 1985 and July 1986.

Telemaque, Eleanor Wong. *It's Crazy to Stay Chinese in Minnesota*. New York: Thomas Nelson, 1978.

Wenquan. "Chinatown Literature During the Last Ten Years (1939–1949)." Translated by Marlon K. Hom. *Amerasia Journal*, Spring/Summer 1982.

Harry Lee, Chinese Cowboy

Chen, Lily Lee. Papers. Chinese Women of America Research Project, Chinese Culture Foundation of San Francisco.

Deputies for Lee in '83. "We Salute You, Sheriff Lee." Advertisement. *New Orleans Times Picayune*, April 29, 1983.

Eig, Jonathan, and Fitzgerald, Tom. "Lee Aide Making Sure Order Is Understood." *New Orleans Times Picayune*, December 10, 1986.

Eig, Jonathan. "Lee Tries to Calm Storm." *New Orleans Times Picayune*, December 5, 1986.

Eig, Jonathan. "Lee: Will Stop Blacks in White Areas." *New Orleans Times Picayune*, December 3, 1986.

Eig, Jonathan, and Ross, Bob. "Lee Withdraws Plan to Stop Blacks." *New Orleans Times Picayune*, December 4, 1986.

Eig, Jonathan. "NAACP Calls for Lee's Resignation." *New Orleans Times Picayune*. December 8, 1986.

Eig, Jonathan. "Oust Lee, Angry Blacks Say." *New Orleans Times Picayune*, December 8, 1986.

Eig, Jonathan. "Time Tempers Residents' Views of Lee's Order." *New Orleans Times Picayune*, January 11, 1986.

Hsu, Evelyn. "Influx of Asians Stirs Up Los Angeles Area's 'Little Taipei.'" *San Francisco Chronicle*, August 1, 1986.

Harrison, Laird. "Killer Goes Free." *Asian Week*, May 8, 1981.

Infocom Broadcast Services. "The American Character, with Norman Vincent Peale." Typescript #1719, Program #1657.

Lee, Harry. Interview with author. New Orleans, Louisiana, May 1986.

McKendall, Rhonda. "Jeff Urged to Reject Sheriff's Statements." *New Orleans Times Picayune*. December 13, 1986.

Nolan, Bruce. "Lee: Defending the Indefensible." *New Orleans Times Picayune*, March 23, 1985.

Nolan, Bruce. "Sheriff Practices Damage Control." *New Orleans Times Picayune*, December 13, 1986.

Ross, Bob. "Fire Steals Christmas, But Not Families' Spirit." *New Orleans Times Picayune*, December 26, 1983.

Shiffman, James R. "Chinese-Americans: Many—But Far from All—Push Upward." *San Diego Union*, September 9, 1979.

(Unknown.) "Christmas Spirit Finally Catches Up with Fire Victims." *New Orleans Times Picayune*, January 12, 1984.

(Unknown.) "Don't Just Condemn Lee for Remarks, Rights Officials Urge." *New Orleans Times Picayune*, January 12, 1984.

(Unknown.) "First Chinese American Political Action Committee Meets in Los Angeles." *Asian Week*, October 21, 1983.

Viviano, Frank. "The Long March to City Hall." *Image Magazine*, *San Francisco Examiner*, May 11, 1986.

Young, Kris. "Southern Sheriff: The Unfinished Saga of Harry Lee." *Jade*, Winter 1982.

Adrienne Telemaque Versus Suzie Wong

Chan, Jeffrey Paul; Chin, Frank; Inada, Lawson; and Wong, Shawn. "Resources for Chinese and Japanese American Literary Traditions." *Amerasia Journal*, Spring/Summer 1981.

Chin, Frank. "Interview: Roland Winters." *Amerasia Journal*, Fall 1973.

Cummings, Hildegard, and Terenzio, Stephanie, ed. *The Paintings of Yun Gee*. The William Benton Museum of Art, 1979.

Deng, Ming-Dao. Interview with author. San Francisco, California, February 1985.

Eng, Dr. Tony. Interview with author. Freehold, New Jersey, July 1986.

Fong-Torres, Ben. "Why There Are No Male Asian Anchors." *Datebook, San Francisco Chronicle,* July 13, 1986.

Freedman, Samuel G. "Debate Persists on Minority Casting." *New York Times,* August 22, 1984.

Gok, Forrest. Interview with author. San Francisco, California, February 1985.

Kim, Elaine H. *With Silk Wings.* Oakland: Asian Women United, 1982.

Lee, Bobbie. "Asians Seen as Work Horses Instead of Racers, Lam Says." *Asian Week,* May 22, 1987.

Schwartz, John, with Raine, George, and Robins, Kate. "A 'Super-minority' Tops Out." *Newsweek,* May 11, 1987.

Stone, Judy. "He Pictures the Chinese with 'A Bit of Heart.'" *San Francisco Chronicle,* August 25, 1985.

Telemaque, Adrienne. Interview with author. New York City, July 1986.

Telemaque, Eleanor Wong. Interview with author. New York City, July 1986.

Wang, Caroline. "White 'Asians' Back in Movies." *Asian Week,* July 5, 1986.

Wong, Yen Lu. "Chinese-American Theatres." *Drama Review,* July 1976.

Young, Rebecca. Interview with author. San Francisco, California. June 1987.

Yu, Connie Young. *Profiles in Excellence: Peninsula Chinese Americans.* Stanford Area Chinese Club, 1986.

Pamela Wong and Her Search for Roots

Chan, Marcia Jean, and Chan, Candice Cynda, eds. *Going Back.* San Francisco: self-published, 1973.

Jeung, Russell. "Chinese Americans in China." *A Thousand Voices,* Spring 1987.

Wong, Pamela. "Chinatown's Beginning: An Oral History of Portland." Paper, Lewis and Clark College, 1986.

Wong, Pamela. Interview with author. Portland, Oregon, September 1986.

Wong, Pamela. Journal of Pamela Wong. Portland, Oregon.

Wong, Pamela. Letters to author, 1986 and 1987.

Ho Yuet Fung, Immigrant

Adams, Gerald. "Dispelling the Myths about Chinatown." *San Francisco Examiner and Chronicle,* August 10, 1980.

Chaw, Gladys. Interview with author. San Francisco, June 1987.

Chen, Serena. "Suicide and Depression Identified as Serious Problems for Asian Youth." *East/West News,* April 9, 1987.

Glynn, Thomas, and Wang, John. "Chinatown." *Neighborhood,* December 1978.

Ho, Yuet Fung. Interview with author. New York City, June 1986.

Itow, Laurie. "Hong Kong's Quiet Bay Area Presence." *San Francisco Examiner,* June 7, 1987.

Jung, Henry. "Freckled Rice Provides a Compassionate Look at Being Young and Chinese American." *Sampan,* August 19, 1983.

Jung, Henry. "Stephen C. Ning Talks about His New Film." *Sampan,* August 19, 1983.

Laundry Workers. Papers. New York Chinatown History Project.

Ning, Stephen. Interview with author. New York City, June 1986.

(Unknown.) "Asian Immigrants Say Schoolmates Harass Them." *San Francisco Chronicle,* March 28, 1987.

(Unknown.) "Works in Progress: An Interview with Stephen Ning." *Cinevue,* April 1986.

Yu, Renqiu. Interview with author. New York City, June 1986.

Some Major Legislation Affecting Chinese in America

Asian Pacific American Coalition. *Alert* (Newsletter). June 1986, August 1986, November 1986.

Briscoe, Edward Eugene. "Pershing's Chinese Refugees: An Odyssey of the Southwest." Master's thesis, St. Mary's University, San Antonio, Texas, 1947.

Chapin, Frederic L. "Homer Lea and The Chinese Revolution." Thesis, Harvard University, 1950.

Glick, Carl. *Double Ten: Captain O'Banion's Story of the Chinese Revolution.* New York: Whittlesey House, 1945.

Fay, Yolanda Cantalupi. Papers of Rosemarie Fay Loomis, New Orleans, Louisiana.

Harrison, Laird. "Experts Estimate Up to 175,000 Asian Illegal Aliens." *Asian Week,* May 29, 1987.

Hendricks, Bill. "Blackjack Pershing and the Chinese Texans." *San Antonio Express,* April 21, 1985.

Kim, Hyung-chan, ed. *Dictionary of Asian American History.* Westport: Greenwood Press, 1986.

Lai, Him Mark and Choy, Philip P. *Outlines: History of the Chinese in America.* San Francisco: self-published, 1971.

Loomis, Rosemarie Fay. Interview with author. New Orleans, Louisiana, May 1986.

McCunn, Ruthanne Lum. *An Illustrated History of the Chinese in America.* San Francisco: Design Enterprises of San Francisco, 1979.

Nee, Victor G., and de Bary, Brett. *Longtime Californ': A Documentary Study of an American Chinatown.* Boston: Houghton Mifflin Co., 1974.

Nims, Amy Elizabeth. "Chinese Life in San Antonio." Master's thesis, Southwest Texas State Teachers College, San Marcos, Texas, 1941.

Sanger, Carol. "Fear of Family Separation Undermining Immigration Act." *East/West News,* September 10, 1987.

Tung, William L. *The Chinese in America 1820–1973: A Chronology and Fact Book.* Dobbs Ferry: Oceana Publications, Inc. 1974.

(Unknown.) "Uncle Sam Moves Chinese Village to Camp Wilson." *San Antonio Express,* June 8, 1917.

(Unknown.) "Wives of Two Chinese Regain U.S. Citizenship." *Detroit Free Press,* July 21, 1931.

Worley, F. B. "Five Hundred Chinese Refugees." *Overland Monthly,* April 1918.

Yung, Judy. "Chinese-American Woman Opened the Doors for Others." *Oakland Tribune,* December 7, 1986.

A NOTE ON TRANSLITERATION

Spoken Chinese varies according to dialect but the written language is the same. So Mandarin and Cantonese speakers who cannot understand each other verbally can communicate through the written characters. Transliteration into the Roman alphabet, however, depends on sound. Through the years, different systems have been devised, none of them entirely satisfactory. The most recent is Pinyin.

Developed in China during the 1950s, Pinyin conforms to the Mandarin dialect and is currently used by the official Chinese news agency and prominent Western newspapers and journals. Nevertheless, to spare the reader unnecessary confusion, I have kept the old familiar spellings for places: Canton, not Guangzhou. The majority of Chinese Americans trace their ances-try to southern China, and their names have been Romanized according to southern dialects, including Cantonese, Toishanese, Lungdo, Hakka, and Sunwui, to name just a few. Traditionally, a Chinese name begins with the surname. But a few Chinese Americans follow the Western style of placing the surname at the end. The Chinese given name is usually two syllables, each represented by a character. To denote this, some Chinese Americans hyphenate the Romanization, others run the Romanization together into a single word, and still others separate the Romanization into two words. There are also many who have English given names and Chinese surnames. In each instance, I have respected the choices made by the individual; the resulting variations reflect the diversity that is Chinese America.

ADDITIONAL PERMISSIONS

Chew Law Ying and her daughter, Bick Heung, epigraph, page 11, Courtesy Tom Bick Fong

Chinese section hands eating, page 18, Courtesy The Montana Historical Society, Helena, Montana

Ko Kun Hua and Ko Kun Hua's children, page 20, by permission of the Harvard University Archives

Chinese Educational Mission baseball team, page 22, Courtesy Historical Photograph Collections, Washington State University Library, Pullman

Yale Rowing Team, page 22, Courtesy Yale University Archives, Yale University Library

Surviving Central Pacific Railroad Workers, page 49, Courtesy Brininstool Collection, Amon Carter Museum, Fort Worth, Texas

Ing Hay and Lung On, page 56, Leah Hing, page 94, Chinese War Brides, page 149, Courtesy Oregon Historical Society, negative numbers 26468, 53840 238-A, ORH58757, 58758 238-A

"Whoopee Review," page 136, Courtesy Billy Rose Theatre Collection, The New York Public Library at Lincoln Center, Astor, Lenox and Tilden Foundations

Wong Chin Foo, page 175, Courtesy Chin Foo Collection

ACKNOWLEDGEMENTS

This book was completed with the help of numerous friends and strangers who made my interests theirs. To all the individuals and institutions credited as sources for photographs and information—especially those people who generously shared their personal stories—I give my heartfelt thanks.

The knowledge and insights gained from a trip to Toishan, China, at the beginning of this project are reflected in much of this work. I am indebted to the people at Flower City Publishing, the China International Exchange Centre, and the Overseas Chinese Affairs Office of Toishan, who made the journey possible.

Judy Yung and Him Mark Lai saved me months of work by sharing materials from their own files. Discussions with them helped me develop my ideas, and their critical readings of several drafts helped me shape the book. For their many contributions I am deeply grateful.

Though not named directly as sources, Ron Chew, Dan Connerton, Henry Der, Amy Jean Hanscom, Silas Jue, Dr. Thomas Q. Kong, Mrs. Chih Meng, John H. Plumb, Sanford M. Plumb, Theresa Lupica Poss, Dr. Raymond T. Rufo, C. Y. Shu, Audrey Sweeney, Sidney Taylor, and Maxine Turner were helpful in providing insights and obtaining crucial pieces of information, and I give them my thanks.

I appreciate the cooperation of the following institutions and collections not otherwise acknowledged: Augusta Regional Library, Armistad Research Center, Bancroft Library at the University of California at Berkeley, Georgia Historical Society, Hawaiian Collection at the University of Hawaii Library, Historic Augusta, San Francisco Public Library, and the Louisiana Collection at Tulane University Library.

Particular librarians, archivists, and curators whose interest and assistance went beyond their job descriptions were: Marilyn Kwock, Alaska Historical Library; Heather S. Hatch, Arizona Historical Society; Wei-Chi Poon, Asian American Studies Library at the University of California at Berkeley; Deborah Dunn, Bishop Museum; Eric Paddock, Colorado Historical Society; Ruth Blair, Connecticut Historical Society; Beverly McFarland, Eugene C. Barker Texas History Center at the University of Texas; Sally Mosely, Georgia Department of Archives and History; Robin Carlaw, Harvard University Archives; Kellye Magee, Pamela D. Arceneaux, and Jessica Travis, Historic New Orleans Collection; Carolyn Micnhimer, Kam Wah Chung Museum; Rose Lambert, Louisiana State Museum; Dan Den Bleyker and Forrest W. Galey, Mississippi Department of Archives and History; Wayne Everard, New Orleans Public Library; Joyce Justice, National Archives, Seattle Branch; Charlie Lai, New York Chinatown History Project; Lisa Jarish, North Adams Public Library; Louisa Kilgroe, North Carolina China Council; Philip Richart, Oregon Military Museum; Beverly Byrd, State Library of Florida; Dorothy Minor, Stetson University; Richard J. Viet, Texas Collection, Baylor University; William K. Jolley, Uintah County Library; Linda Thatcher, Utah State Historical Society; Tom Joynes, Virginia Military Institute; and Tad Russell, Washington County Library System. In a few instances, the material I sought was not found, but this in no way diminishes my appreciation.

I also wish to thank; Michael Collette and Philip Choy for reproducing some of the photographs; David Barich and Robin Grossman for helping with the photo selection; Marlon Hom for his advice and his translations of documents from Chinese; Catherine Brady, Rita Drysdale, Harry Lawton, Lillian Louie, Diane Mark, George Ow, Jr., Jack Tchen, Tsai Nuliang, Jan Venolia, and Yu Renqiu for their thoughtful criticisms; Ellen Yeung for helping formulate a policy for the Romanizations; and Jay Schaefer for his keen editorial eye and excellent advice.

But, as always, my largest debt is to my husband, who has helped at every stage of the project. Without his active support and substantial contributions this book would not have been completed.

Index